The URBAN RAJAH's CURRY MEMOIRS

IVOR PETERS

headline

First published in Great Britain in 2013
by HEADLINE PUBLISHING GROUP

1

Cataloguing in Publication Data is available
from the British Library

Hardback ISBN 978 0 7553 64039

Typeset in Fairfield Light and Copperplate Gothic

Printed and bound in Great Britain by
Butler Tanner & Dennis

Headline's policy is to use papers that
are natural, renewable and recyclable
products and made from wood grown
in sustainable forests. The logging and
manufacturing processes are expected
to conform to the environmental
regulations of the country of origin.

HEADLINE PUBLISHING GROUP
An Hachette UK Company
338 Euston Road
London NW1 3BH

www.headline.co.uk
www.hachette.co.uk

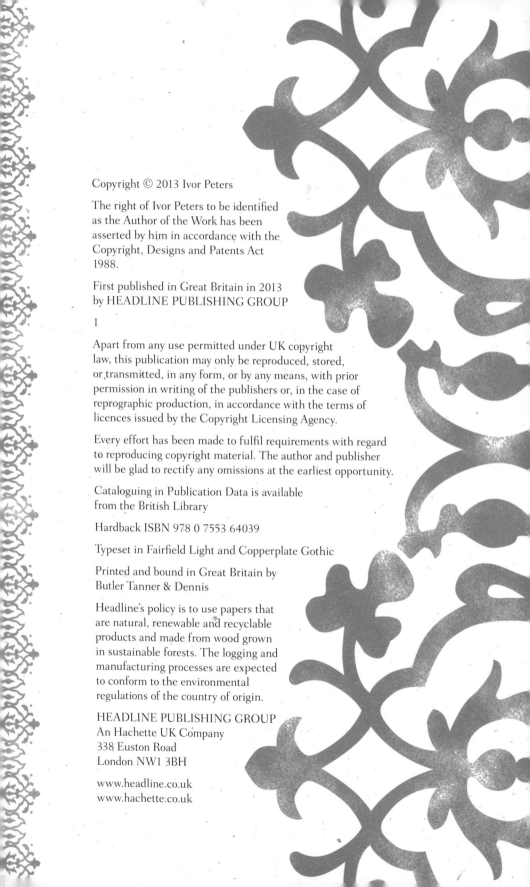

This book is dedicated to those
who have inspired me to be more;
Jeanne, Florence, Victor,
Nana George and Ian.

The Urban Rajah as a boy

THE URBAN RAJAH

The Urban Rajah is a food author, cook, traveller and lifestyle adventurer with roots deep in the Indian subcontinent. A son of 1970s Britain, he grew up on hot summers, street cricket and spiced Indian food. Terraced living was shared with his brother, mother, father and a pair of orange curtains.

His celebrated blog www.urbanrajah.com is dedicated to spiced recipes and stories about food, travel, life and style finds.

The Urban Rajah grew up on fish fingers and baked beans whilst also tearing up hot chapattis and scooping vivid spiced curry made from family recipes that had passed through three generations and crossed three continents. He adores the home-cooked spiced food – influenced by the East and married with Western cuisine – that represents his immigrant roots. Family gatherings were central to his early life. Speakers the size of sofas would throb to the beat of ska, reggae and bhangra and that's where he traces his passion for music, and probably explains his vinyl collection, the club nights and his spell as a pirate radio DJ.

He runs the elusive and highly acclaimed pop-up restaurant Cash n Curry, a social enterprise dedicated to raising funds for projects helping India's street children. Known for his high-energy persona and uplifting style, he frequently demonstrates his passion for Indian bazaar cuisine at food festivals.

A self-confessed dandy, he rarely leaves home without a tub of moustache wax or a piece of headwear. That's the Urban Rajah.

OVERVIEW

The chapatti shuffle is an exceptional manoeuvre.

It requires dexterity, loose shoulders, a wobbly head and dry hands. It's one of my earliest memories of growing up in Slough, a town that defines multiculturalism. I would perch on the kitchen step watching my grandparents perform this routine, their shoulders shimmying as they flick-flacked plate-sized balls of floury unleavened dough, producing cartoon-size clouds. The result was heavenly, fresh, hot chapattis straight off the tawa (frying pan) and brushed with a thin layer of butter. The taste is an evocative one and even now, as I write this, I'm transported back to my childhood, where I first fell in love with curry.

Everything was fresh back then. The blended spices seemed to possess magical properties to charm the nose and the colours glowed brilliantly. The dishes we ate at home were special; they'd passed through generations and made it to the 1970s – a decade that saw us wearing bad trousers, owning a Datsun Sunny and hanging tangerine orange curtains in our window bay. It was a time when pineapples were a novelty and avocado bathroom suites were all the rage; an era where taste had packed its suitcase and gone AWOL.

Fortunately this never seemed to apply to the food we ate. My family were inventive with the ingredients they'd hunted down, so

weekend gatherings were turned into gastronomic feasts. Sail-like sheets would carpet the dining-room floor in swathes of vivid red, yellow and green, creating a feasting table fit for twenty where we'd sit cross-legged, inhaling the delicious promise breezing through from the kitchen. The crowning glories of these occasions were the signature dishes cooked by the men in the family. These men were brothers – my father, Victor Peters; Guddu Chachu (Uncle Stan); Lawrie Uncle (Uncle Lawrence), and Uncle Abbu (Uncle Albert).

When the brothers arrived in England they started cooking out of necessity, spurred on by a large dose of homesickness, and a small pinch of fear – the thought of yet another Spam fritter in Blighty. In those early carefree years, we kids took their cooking for granted. It was what we were used to, fabulous food that left your lips tingling and begging for more. But now I can see that this early introduction to the food of my forefathers was a gift.

Back then they were young with jet black hair, smooth brown skin and a zest for life. Decades on, their eyes sparkle with the wisdom of age, their hair has turned silver and the years have produced crow's feet. Their cooking, however, is as good, or even better. In my opinion they are the definition of Old Spice and it's their food which has motivated me to cook, write about and host subcontinent Indian feasts fit for a Rajah.

Compelled to capture their stories and the food that's narrated our lives, I've written this book. Here are their home-cooked recipes, uncomplicated, practical, clean, honest food inspired by circumstance, history, family break-up, joy and spice. These recipes have traversed continents and travelled through time and they all tell part of a story. My story.

PART ONE
VICTOR PETERS

VICTOR PETERS

Victor Peters had sharp-elbow syndrome.

He was one of seven siblings and mealtimes were like athletics competitions. If you wanted any of the steaming curry on offer, you had to be quick and cunning. He grew up in the 1940s in Karachi, Pakistan, where mealtimes were cherished moments in the post-war Empire. The clan would huddle around age-beaten metal frying pans full of mutton chops draped in clove and coriander gravy, juggling scorching rotis straight from the tandoor. A refreshing salad bursting with plump tomatoes and delicate strands of onion would cool their palates and the ceiling fan would usher out the heat of the day. Fingers dripped with the debris of squishy ripe mangoes, and familiar stories about wrestling matches would be retold by my grandfather, Dhadha-ji.

Food was the central and oldest member of the Peters family and, as in all Asian families, its position was respected. But it wasn't always plentiful, as my father found out when he was packed off as a seven-year-old to board at St Don Bosco Catholic School, Karachi which sounds more like a mafia trattoria than a Franciscan college. Strict 5am starts, serving at mass and carrying out daily chores didn't agree with Dad. He was curious, energetic and hungry … all the time. Frugal meals were served three times a day by a cook who had taken inspiration from a Dickens novel – the food was

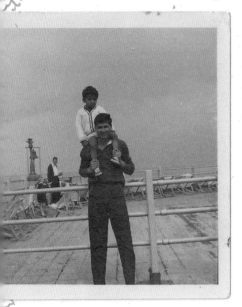

basic and there was never quite enough. Despite being confined to the school compound, on roasting summer days Dad would bunk off, climbing the wall to run to the nearby beach where he'd gulp sea air and appropriate barbecued fish and sweetened corn cobs from their sun-tarred owners. His return from freedom was always greeted by the wicked lick of a cane, but the wonderful taste of spiced liberty justified the Great Escape. He was homesick and sick of the food, but he had seven years of this to endure. Each time he returned to the family nest, Dhadhi-ji, my grandmother, would feed him a drink of crushed almonds and sugared milk to aid his nutritional convalescence, and he still faithfully drinks this today. For our family, food wasn't just functional, it was celebrated.

But Victor's gaze was on distant shores, where adventure beckoned and opportunity abounded. Having grown up in a country that had been under colonial rule for nearly a century, he was keen to explore Britain's green shires and the swinging sixties. In 1962 he arrived in Cambridge, where a bedsit became home. His vision of prosperity soured from rose to grey as, like most immigrants, he was welcomed with a large mug of prejudice and often treated as a second-class citizen, a little like the street hawkers in Karachi were treated. His homesick letters were met with encouragement from his father to stick it out.

When he first arrived in England, Dad cultivated a canned diet – if it came in a can, he'd eat it. Campbell's soup, Heinz varieties, Spam and corned beef all featured regularly. It was a novelty, but a galaxy away from the real food he'd been reared on. Pretty soon, in search of nostalgia, and nourishment, his spice route led him to the International Store, the only grocer in Cambridge to stock curry

powder. Armed with a basket of Eastern ingredients, he set about recalling dishes he'd watched his mother prepare, his body yearning for spice, heat and comforting memories.

Twelve months later he had found work west of London and married my mother, whose charmed existence had left her devoid of any culinary skills. She was more used to the sound of scurrying servants than the hiss of a boiling curry pot. Necessity and teamwork united my father and mother in the kitchen, where they performed their own chapatti shimmy. Spending time on the assembly line in Slough's factories, Dad worked shoulder to shoulder with friends from the old country where they reminisced about food and shared tiffin-style lunch boxes crammed with energy-packed white rice mixed with fiery lentil daal.

Long shifts during the week culminated in Friday nights that exploded to the sounds of Motown as, away from the watchful eye of parents, the skinny Asian twenty-somethings partied, gossiped, traded recipes, ate samosas and explored their new lives.

Years later, my father, by this time estranged from my mother, would find himself in the US in a familiar position of discovery. Thus his food navigates a journey of over 7,000 miles and three continents, and three children and grandchildren. He's been busy, and here's the food that's kept him going. It's not fussy, it's not manicured. It's honest and it's how we eat.

HOME-COMING MILKSHAKE

As a boy my dad would sit counting the beads of condensation as they formed on the glass until they joined and slid down the side like lonesome tears. The milk froth perched above the rim concealed the goodness beneath, a blend of enriching almonds crushed and mixed with whole milk, cardamom and sugar. This was designed by my grandmother to breathe life into my father's nutrition-starved body on his return from his Catholic boarding school. Packed with vitamin E, iron and calcium, this high-energy milkshake represented more than its medicinal properties; it was a metaphor for care, attention and security. In the company of his family he risked nothing but love, starkly in opposition to the promise of pain from the schoolmaster's cane if he dared asked for 'more'. He would watch the tears dripping down the glass, forming a tiny pond at the base, and visualise the contact of the glass of goodness against his lips and the thrill of the ice-cold milk chilling his core as it travelled down his throat, sending involuntary shivers across his shoulders. It would take a matter of seconds to drink so he'd savour the moment before he gulped it down, nutty, sweet and creamy. Finally the moment came and with the thirst of a sailor he would chug it down, finishing off with a milk moustache flourish.

DUDH BADAM (ALMOND MILKSHAKE)

Serves a thirsty 6

2 pints whole milk
8 cardamom pods, cracked, seeds removed
    and ground into powder
10 tsp sugar
20–30 almonds

Simple, quick and energising. Pop everything
in a blender, reserving some cardamom powder,
and blitz, pour into a jug, cover and chill. Stir
and serve, sprinkling the top of the milk with the
reserved cardamom.

SUSTAINING SWEET CHAPATTI MIX

I blame my father, and his father, my Dhadha-ji, for my sweet tooth. Vivid images of the rare treat of churri are seared in my memory. I sat cross-legged on the rug wearing a thick carpet of hair, wild and unmanageable. Dad sat with a mixing bowl in front of him while his fingers went to work like a blender, shredding fresh hot chapattis, lobbing in chunks of butter and sprinkling sugar from on high with the flourish of a wizard distributing magic dust. His spectacles balanced on the bridge of his nose as he inspected his efforts, eyes fixed as his long fingers laboured slowly and methodically, reducing the flatbread and its buddies to juicy morsels of sweetened dough, like a deconstructed doughnut. Deliciously naughty as an adult, but innocently addictive as a child, this is a dish I've never experienced outside our family walls. For my father, it was another sustaining dish for his return from another food-starved term at boarding school. He was skinny and small for his age so my grandparents fed him with churri to fill his frame. I'm aching for another bowl, but strictly for medicinal purposes, of course!

CHURRI

Serves up to 4

400g wholemeal flour, more for dusting
250ml water
200g salted butter, at room temperature
4 tbsp sugar

First, make the chapatti flatbread. Mix the flour and water to create a soft dough, adding a little more flour if it's too sticky. Cover and leave to stand for 30 minutes (overnight is better). Oil your palms and on a flour-dusted surface divide into 8–10 pieces and shape into balls. Flatten with the heel of your palm, then roll them into rounds of 15cm diameter.

Heat a tawa or large heavy frying pan over a high setting and then, when the pan is hot, reduce the heat to medium. One by one, add each chapatti to the pan, cooking for about 20 seconds, using a tea towel to press it lightly until you can feel the heat coming through. Be careful not to press too hard and make it stick to the pan. All you're doing here is making sure the bread is cooked. It'll start to puff and, as soon as it does this, flip it over and do the same again. You're looking for brown, slightly blistered patches. Set aside in a tea towel keeping it hot, and repeat until they're all made.

Tip the chapattis into a large bowl (resist eating them if you can) and start tearing them into tiny pieces. They should still be nice and warm. Slap in the butter and sugar and, using the tips of your fingers, start mincing the ingredients as if rubbing your thumbs across the tops of your fingers with the bread, butter and sugar in the middle. After a few minutes there should be little evidence of the grainy sugar and you'll be staring at a flaky mixture. Decant into small serving bowls.

You can eat it with a fork but I prefer using fingers, pinching morsels in compressed bite-sizes.

'EAT YOUR GREENS'

This is a well-travelled piece of wisdom, dispensed across the kitchen table to reluctant knee-high diners by mothers the world over. But earthy, verdant vegetables held no appeal for Dad and his siblings. Everything had to be meaty or sticky and sweet. Crouching over a small stack of well-worn rupees with gnarled edges, they would count. The tension hung heavy as they worked out whether they had enough money to buy the neon orange syrupy jalebi. Their sisters all tried to guess the result as they examined their brothers' expressions, seeing either wide grins or despondent eyes. My father reflects, 'It's probably a good thing we lacked funds, otherwise I'd have teeth the colour of molasses.'

My grandparents had six mouths to feed, so Dad's childhood meals were sometimes thrifty but always nutritious, and vegetarian dishes featured regularly. This recipe has been customised by Dad to harness iron-packed spinach (palak) and mustard leaves (saag) with a canon of spices prepared quickly and simply. As you munch on the deep green leaves, your senses will applaud your choice and you'll crave just one more morsel. Be careful, though – you could be on your way to becoming a 'greens' junkie.

PALAK SAAG KI SUBZI

Serves 4

1kg fresh saag (mustard leaves)
1kg fresh palak (spinach)
Tadka (see box)
Salt

The secret to this dish is to prepare a delicious tadka (see box) and then add this to the cooked mustard and spinach leaves. You can do this whilst the greens are cooking.

Wash the leaves thoroughly, ridding them of their soil and any companions they've picked up on their journey, then pat them dry. Pick off the stalks and discard them. You'll be left with a hillock of foliage. Chop it roughly.

In a large pan on a low heat, add the leaves, handful by handful, stirring them until they wilt a little and release their water. Throw in a generous pinch of salt and keep agitating until the leaves have dried a little and taken on a British Racing Green tone. Don't let them turn to mush. Now add the tadka and rouse the ingredients for 1 minute until they've combined and acquainted each other.

Serve with chapattis or as a side dish.

VP'S SIMPLE TADKA – NO. 1

Victor's tadka for this dish is speedy and takes little preparation, yet the result leaves me marvelling at its minimalism. The ingredients are humble but manage to charm the spinach and mustard leaves to yield more of their flavour.

2 tbsp olive oil
1 large onion, chopped into small chunks
2 garlic cloves, chopped
5cm fresh root ginger, peeled and chopped
1 long green chilli, sliced
½ tsp brown mustard seeds
Salt and pepper

Put a frying pan over medium heat and add the oil. When hot, pop in the onion and garlic, allowing them to brown and crisp at the edges. Add the ginger, chilli and mustard seeds and turn up the heat a little, until the seeds jig and hop in the pan; season with a little salt and pepper. Fry for a further 3–4 minutes until the ginger has softened and the chilli has turned from green to a dullish brown, then take off the heat and leave to cool.

MAMA PETERS' JHALFREZI

Contrary to popular perception, Asian families have a strong matriarchal line. The women simply let the fellas believe they run the family. Ours was no different.

My grandmother was brought up in a Christian mission orphanage in the province of Uttar Pradesh, north-east India. Mama, or Dhadhi-ji (which means Father's Mother) as we knew her, would prepare this fiery dry-fry dish for my father on his return from school, a dish she claimed to originate from Uttar Pradesh. Others have suggested that it's actually a Bengal dish, as the word *jhal* means hot in Bengali. The ingredients collide in rough chunks and make you want to jam your fingers in and pluck out fat onion-covered peppers. Whoever created this recipe needs to be honoured. Dhadhi-ji made it her own through grinding fresh spices to form a special garam masala. She served this to her children with a healthy measure of fresh green chillies and gorgeous hot chapattis. You can, of course, moderate the heat by reducing the amount of chillies you add but that would be akin to painting a Cheshire Cat grin on the Mona Lisa … a little inappropriate.

Mama's ground garam masala differs slightly from others (see pages 46 and 53) by the addition of fennel. The reason we use whole garam masala as well as the ground version is that the unbroken spices retain an aromatic and subtler finish, contributing elegance rather than adding heat.

JHALFREZI

Serves 4 who like it hot

500g chicken breasts, skinless and boneless, chopped into
    largish chunks
1 tsp ground cumin
1 tsp ground coriander
4 tbsp sunflower or olive oil
1 large red onion, roughly chopped
2.5cm fresh root ginger, peeled and sliced
3 garlic cloves, chopped
6 long thin green chillies, 4 chopped, 2 whole
Whole garam masala – 1 tsp black peppercorns, 1 stick of
    cinnamon, 4 cardamom pods (black)
Salt
1 x 400g tin tomatoes
1 red pepper, chopped
1 green pepper, chopped
2 tsp ground garam masala (see box)
Bunch of fresh coriander, leaves chopped

Coat the chunks of chicken in the cumin and coriander,
cover and stick in the fridge for an hour or so (30 minutes
will do it if you're in a hurry).

In a large frying pan, heat 3 tbsp of the oil on a medium
heat and fry the onion, ginger, garlic and the 4 chopped
green chillies until softened. Pitch in the whole garam masala, turn the heat down to low and add the chicken, and
salt to taste. Keep stirring to ensure it doesn't stick, adding
a little water if required. Cook for a few minutes so that the
chicken feels a little firm, then add the tinned tomatoes
and boil gently for around 15 minutes. Toss in the chopped
peppers and ground garam masala plus the 2 whole chillies

and let it cook for another 5–8 minutes until the pepper softens and the chicken is cooked. Coat with the remaining tablespoon of oil. Add additional water if you want it thinner, but it should have a thick and dense shiny texture. Before serving, fling in the fresh coriander and mix it a little so it releases its fragrance.

Eat with Chapattis (page 172) or rice and a healthy dollop of cool Raitha (page 224).

MAMA'S GROUND GARAM MASALA

This is pretty aromatic and will make a serious impression on its consumers.

1 tsp fennel seeds
½ tsp cumin seeds
1 tsp coriander seeds
¾ tsp crushed bay leaves
1 tsp black peppercorns
4–5 green cardamom pods (or ½ tsp seeds)
4 cloves
4 large black cardamom pods (or ¾ tsp seeds)

Heat a frying pan on a medium heat, then add all the spices. Dry-roast for 2 minutes until they brown and start to scent the room. DON'T burn them. Leave to cool. Peel the cardamom pods and release the seeds into the other spices, tip into a pestle and mortar (or blender) and blast them.

Mama's ground Garam Masala

1 tsp fennel seeds
½ tsp cumin seeds
1 tsp coriander seeds
3/4 tsp crushed bay leaves
1 tsp black peppercorns
4-5 green cardam
(or ½

BABA THE STREET CHEF
IN KARACHI

The greying chef was well groomed and had served generations of hungry diners at his streetside serving hatch. He had slicked-back hair, a trimmed and manicured silver moustache, nimble fingers and a white apron sporting bloodied spatters in the style of a Jackson Pollock masterpiece. His long heavy knife glistened and, with menacing accuracy, tap-danced across the granite slab. Behind him fire flared from burners while spice-oiled skillets cackled and hissed as he tipped the contents from the chopping stones into the pans. Dad watched the men queue, clutching bowls filled with maroon-coloured meat, waiting their turn for an earthy meal to be created at the hands of Baba the chef. The sharp clatter of steel against stone clacked *kata-kut, kata-kut, kata-kut,* christening the dish with its affectionate name. The smell was unlike any Dad had known: heady, masculine, brave, notes of musk with bursts of fresh green chilli and ginger. As different shapes and textures of meat went into the pans, curiosity gripped Dad and he enquired of Baba as to the contents. His inquisition was greeted with a laugh and Baba pointed to various body parts, heart, liver and kidney. Dad was horrified, but he acquiesced and tried a chunk from Baba's knife – intensely rich and packed with life. Like his first sip of beer, he knew he was experiencing the palate of an adult. He was intrigued by this delicacy as a boy and his version is pared back to its pauper-chic roots. It's bold, unapologetic and utterly visceral.

Serve with Raitha (page 224) and Chapattis (page 172).

KATA KUT

Serves 4

500g lamb or chicken liver

2 lamb kidneys

1 lamb or beef heart

3 lemons: juice 1 and halve
the remaining 2

1 lamb brain (optional but try
an Asian butcher)

3 tbsp olive oil

1 onion, finely sliced

4 tomatoes, finely chopped

2 tbsp ginger paste (see page
93)

1 tbsp garlic paste (see page
93)

4 green chillies, chopped

2 tsp cumin seeds

1 tsp fennel seeds

2 tsp whole coriander seeds

1 tsp ground garam masala,
either use Mama's recipe
or buy a packet (see page
21)

1 tsp ground cinnamon

Salt and pepper

Large bunch of coriander
leaves, chopped

Roughly chop up the liver, kidneys and heart. Squish the lemon juice over them and set aside. If using lamb brain, cook for 3 minutes in a pan of boiling water, then discard the water, chop roughly and leave to cool. Meanwhile, in a large frying pan, warm the oil over a medium heat and drop in the onion, frying until golden around the edges. Add the tomatoes and cook for a couple of minutes. Add the ginger, garlic, chillies, cumin, fennel and coriander seeds, garam masala, cinnamon and seasoning, and stir to coat everything until a slight paste starts to form, without allowing it to stick. Pop in the lemon halves, heart, kidneys and liver, and cook for 15 minutes. If using lamb brain, pop it in now and cook for another 5 minutes. Drop in the chopped coriander leaves at the last minute and stir, bruising the leaves until they yield their aroma. Serve hot, immediately.

WELCOME

PAPRIKA

MELANGE PAELLA

SAFRAN

MELANGE COUSCOUS

RAS EL HANOUT

GINGEMBRE

HARISSA

MELANGE TAG

BAZAAR FOOD

The morning air was filled with the smell of sizzling platters on an industrial scale, a mix of sugar syrup, fat sultanas and freshly churned butter sweetening the high-octane fumes of rush-hour auto-rickshaws and Ambassador taxis. Horse-drawn carriages, 'tongas', clip-clopped alongside battalions of cyclists and motorists as boys scampered to school in newly pressed white shirts, a short-trousered version of their fathers who clambered through the throng of the city's commuters. Social classes were distinguished by the mode of transport chosen for the morning dash to work, but soon levelled at the food bazaar. Here, amongst the vast open-air food hustlers, men sat cheek by jowl fuelling on food from the bazaar, for breakfast, lunch or dinner. It was a place where social fripperies were cast aside in favour of one thing only … the search for the tastiest *khana* (food). Large-scale hotplates hissed and blistered under the street cooks' commands, doubling up as communal dining tables, where my dad stood or sat with other diners scoffing Indian fast food. Cooks belted out their menus above the din of traffic, cajoling hungry customers to eat at their hotplate. *'Aja nashtar!'* (Come, breakfast is ready!) Suits, flowing salwar kameez, short-sleeved shirts, T-shirts and oil stained overalls all joined the convocation of young and old to devour halwa poori (sweetened semolina and light fried flatbread), aloo chole bathura (spiced potato and chickpea snack with small fried rounds of bread), naan kebab (lamb seekh kebab and naan with chutney) and aloo tikki (potato cutlets), all washed down with sweet milky masala chai. This is industrious food, it built a nation on the move, fuelled their daily ambitions and it's begging to be eaten again.

HALWA AND POORI

To every story, there are always two sides. It's the same with this semolina recipe. Some might think of school dinners from a bygone era, but this dish couldn't be further from those institutional stodge mountains. It has two sides, because whilst it's graced with pistachios, almonds and sultanas – all power packed and healthy – it fraternises with its naughtier cousins sugar, cream and butter. But hey, it's not like this dish is likely to replace your granola and yoghurt breakfast. It's an indulgence that makes life taste just a little sweeter, especially with soft poori in the palm.

HALWA

Serves up to 6

150g medium-coarse semolina
200ml double cream or
　　buttermilk
1 tbsp sultanas
150g sugar

900ml water
250g butter
50g mixed flaked almonds
　　and lightly crushed
　　pistachios, for dusting

In a large bowl mix the semolina, cream and sultanas, and leave to stand for an hour. Over a low heat, mix the sugar and water, stirring gently until the sugar has dissolved and the water has become syrupy.

In a deep pan, heat the butter until it froths, but don't burn it. Add the semolina and cook for around 4–6 minutes, stirring continuously as you don't want it to get lumpy. Pour in the sugar syrup and cook for a further 5 minutes, continuing to stir until the semolina has soaked up the golden butter and is gorgeously tanned. Take it off the heat and dust with the mixed nuts.

Eat hot, either with a poori (page 28) or on its own with a big spoon.

POORI

Makes 8–10

500g wholemeal flour, plus a little extra for dusting
Salt
Water, enough to make a stiff dough
6–8 tbsp vegetable oil

Combine the flour, a pinch of salt and the water in a large mixing bowl to create a malleable (not sticky) dough. Knead on a floured surface until it's really workable, around 5–10 minutes, and then store it in a greased bowl, covering it with a damp tea towel, for at least an hour.

Work the dough over again, then tear off peach-sized pieces, creating 8–10 dough balls. Roll each into a circle, around 15cm in diameter. Using a large frying pan or wok, heat the oil until hot enough to brown a crouton. When the crouton is sizzling and crisp, slide in one poori at a time. Fry for a couple of minutes until it puffs up and turns a deliciously honeyed tone. Remove and drain on kitchen paper, then rip it up and dig into the halwa.

BREAKFAST LIKE A RAJAH

As the saying goes, breakfast like a king, lunch like a prince and dine like a pauper, and it's a recipe like this that'll keep you firing on all cylinders for the morning. If you really can't sacrifice the soft-boiled eggs and soldiers, then consider aloo chole (pronounced 'cholay') as a brunch treat or a snack. It can be reheated in a flash, and coupled with a supple bread bathura will encourage you to banish any rice cake distractions for ever.

ALOO CHOLE

Serves 4

500g potatoes, peeled and diced
1 onion, sliced
2cm fresh root ginger, peeled and finely chopped
2 tbsp vegetable oil
1 tsp ground cumin
1 tsp turmeric
½ tsp chilli powder
½ tsp garam masala (see page 46)
240g drained canned chickpeas
Salt
1 lemon, halved
1 finely chopped tomato, to garnish (optional)

In a pot of salted boiling water, cook the potatoes until soft but not mushy, about 20 minutes. Whilst the potatoes are simmering, take a large frying pan and over a medium heat fry the onions and ginger in the oil until browned and slightly crispy. Add the cumin, turmeric, chilli powder and garam masala to the pan, where they will soak up the other ingredients. Stir for a couple of minutes. Add the chickpeas and thrash them around with the spices, coating everything, then turn the heat down to low and cook for 5–6 minutes until the chickpeas have heated through and softened. Remove from the heat. Once the potatoes are ready, drain and add to the chickpeas, returning to the heat. Season with salt and squeeze in the lemon juice. Stir thoroughly and serve hot, dressed with the chopped tomato, if you like. Eat with a fresh bathura.

BATHURA

Makes 12–14

150ml natural yoghurt (I like to use one with 10% fat)
2 tsp sugar
200ml water
500g plain flour, plus a little more for dusting
120g fine semolina
½ tsp baking powder
Pinch of bicarbonate of soda
Touch of salt
2 tbsp vegetable oil

You'll need a few bowls for this bread mix. Mix the yoghurt, sugar and water in a bowl and leave to rest whilst you crack on with the flour. In a separate bowl, mix the flour, semolina, baking powder, bicarbonate of soda and salt. Make a crater in the middle and pour in the yoghurt mix. Work into a soft dough, turn it on to a floured surface and knead in the oil, continuing to knead for around 10 minutes until it's like a smooth, misshapen bowling ball. If it's too wet, add a little more flour. Grease a bowl and pop in the dough, covering it with a damp tea towel. If you're in a hurry leave it for 15–20 minutes whilst you read the paper.

If you've a mañana approach to cooking, leave it in a warm place overnight.

Oil your palms and tear off an avocado-sized piece of dough. On the floured deck, flatten it and roll it into a circle of 15cm diameter. In a wok or deep frying pan, glug in enough oil to deep-fry the bathura rounds. Test it's hot enough with a small cube of bread: if it sizzles and turns brown quickly it's ready. Carefully slide a bathura in and fry until it's puffed up like a hot water bottle and brown on both sides. Use a slotted spoon to remove it. Drain the bathura on kitchen paper and slip another into the wok. Serve hot and puffy.

BATHURA.

MAKES 12-14

150 ML NATURAL YOGHURT
2 TSP SUGAR
200 ML WATER
500G PLAIN FLOUR + MORE
FOR DUSTING
120G FINE SEMOLINA
½ TSP BAKING POWDER
PINCH OF BICARB OF
TOUCH OF

THE CHAI WALLAH

It's the clarion call of the food bazaar. It can be heard on train platforms, at bus stations, on the street outside offices. It's the distinctive cry of the chai wallah, tempting a thirsty population to slake their longing and sup the milky, sugary, spice-scented tea. It's as institutional as the British monarch, but a bit more available.

MASALA CHAI

Makes 8 cups

2 pints milk
2½ pints water
2cm fresh root ginger, peeled and finely chopped
10 green cardamom pods, crushed
6 cloves, coarsely ground

1 tsp ground fennel seeds
1 cinnamon quill
3 standard teabags (use English Breakfast if in doubt)
Sugar to taste

Heat the milk, water, ginger and spices in a pan, letting it simmer rather than boil over for about 15 minutes until the volume has reduced a little. The liquid will smell deliciously fragrant and you'll be gagging to sip it. Take off the heat and drop in the teabags, allowing the tea to brew for a couple of minutes, or longer if you like it stronger. Strain through a sieve into tea glasses or cups and sweeten according to your taste.

THE MOST REFINED ACCOMPANIMENT

Aged five, sitting cross-legged alongside my brother in our sitting room in Slough, on a dhurrie rug woven in Pakistan with soft cotton strands of rich pink, green, yellow, red, white and orange, I would watch the ceremony of dinner being served, as Dad brought in a series of steamy-lidded dishes in shiny little steel pots, proudly glinting and reflecting the colour of the walls. Mum battled with the heavy orange curtains, pushing them back to give the day its last chance of bathing our living room in light, and checking that we'd scrubbed our hands of the day's sport. Dad balanced glasses, plates, jugs and a little stainless steel container with the dexterity of an octopus.

Mum would ladle out thick spoonfuls of lamb and potatoes, and mixed vegetable subzi coated in a dilution of oil and juice from plum tomatoes. The smell promised sustenance and seconds. Chapattis were handed out and then Dad would uncap the little steel container and liberate the bouquet of onion, lemon, lime, coriander and the sharp mix of thinned vinegar. Carefully placing the container away from any disturbance, he would use a triangle of chapatti to spoon out the raw and fresh vegetables on to the side of his plate. I'd watch Dad's sideburns wobble as he cooled his mouth with the chilli salsa chaser. I'd mimic his facial expression of delight, but it took years before I actually realised that Kachumbar is possibly the most refined accompaniment to curry cuisine. Simple flavours, an elegant finish and easy preparation mean you'll want this dish by your side at every sitting.

KACHUMBAR

Serves 4 as an accompaniment

2 small red onions
3 tomatoes
½ cucumber
1 long green chilli
Small bunch of coriander

For the dressing

1 tsp white wine vinegar
1 tsp sugar
Pinch of salt
1 tbsp lemon juice
1 tbsp lime juice
2 tsp olive oil

I use red onions as they carry a more refined flavour when eaten raw. Chop them into mini cubes. Dice the tomatoes together with their seeds and juice. Cut the cucumber into small pieces, then take the chilli, discard the seeds and finely slice the green skin. Thoroughly wash the coriander, remove the leaves and chop them with care. Mix all the ingredients in a bowl (I use a metal one out of nostalgia), cover and refrigerate for up to an hour.

Put all the dressing ingredients in a bowl and whisk together until combined. Cover and leave at room temperature, allowing the various flavours to blend. When you're ready to eat, jostle the salsa ingredients to aerate them, trickle the dressing all over it and muddle the mixture. It should glisten and shine as a proud companion to any dish.

BRUNCH PARATHAS

They say the sins of the father are visited on their children, and it's this particular naughty inherited indulgence that I hold aloft with pride. It carried me through childhood, adolescence and now into adulthood. Often you hear people discussing the eating habits of their elders and exclaiming how 'A full English breakfast never did my granddad Jim any harm. He ate one every day until he passed away at the age of ninety-three.' In our family the equivalent is the paratha. Dad would trough his way through a stack of them, lips and fingers smacked with the buttery sheen of freshly cooked unleavened bread stuffed with a smooth, spiced potato mixture, his eyes glowing with boyhood delight, nodding in silence as if agreeing with the inner voice of his taste buds yelling for *just another*.

Treated as savoury interruption to the day, I remember parathas as a Saturday treat, where the mornings stretched a little longer and our stomachs yawned for the gut-busting taste of buttered chapattis enveloping the potato masala. The flatbreads were gently fried on a tawa until they scalded a little and took on the appearance of giraffe skin. After being left to cool a while, allowing the parathas to crisp up, we'd sink our teeth into cumin, chilli and turmeric-spiced potato mash wrapped in pan-toasted bread and race to see who could eat the most. I barely managed three, a gargantuan effort, but I was always eclipsed by my brother and father who seemed to tuck them into secret and separate bellies, notching up five or six in a session. These were our brunch snack after Saturday morning telly, where the presenters hammed up their personas in the drive to wake up a slumbering nation. Not much has changed since, only these days the fat handkerchiefs of savoury bread soak up more than just my appetite particularly after a thirsty night out!

PARATHAS

Makes 10–12

500g wholemeal flour, plus a little extra for dusting
Salt
Water, enough to make a stiff dough
300g Aloo Ki Burtha (page 60), minus the tomatoes, mashed
4 tbsp vegetable oil

Sift the flour into a bowl and sprinkle in a pinch of salt, adding a few tablespoons of water to create a stiff-ish dough. If you have time, cover and refrigerate for around 20 minutes. On a floured surface, knead the dough for a few minutes until the mix has become drier and isn't sticky. Snatch away lemon-sized pieces of the dough, shape into balls and dust in flour. This quantity should make around 10–12. Place each little mound on the floury surface and, using a rolling pin, shape into a square approx. 15–20cm on each side. (A tip: make sure the outer edges are thinner than the middle of the square.) Take a tablespoon of the potato filling, drop it in the middle and spread it with the back of the spoon. Now fold each corner of the square into the middle, forming an envelope. Seal the edges with a little water if needed. Flatten again with the rolling pin back to its previous size. Heat a tawa or frying pan over a medium heat and brown one side of the paratha for around 30–40 seconds or until you can feel the heat coming through the other side. Flip over and do exactly the same with the other side. Add a little oil into the pan and shallow-fry both sides of the paratha until it's taken on a rich golden treacle colour. Remove and preserve their heat in a warmed oven, or get someone else on paratha duty whilst you polish off yours fresh from the tawa, either on its own or stung with a sharp mango or lime pickle.

IMPROVISING IN CAMBRIDGE

Simplicity was often the main ingredient in Dad's childhood dining repertoire, which was fuelled by the family's extensive kitchen garden tended by Dhadhi-ji's careful hands.

Tomatoes were reddened by the sun's kisses, chillies hung in slender bunches, okra extended their skinny fingers, potatoes multiplied like an underground army and deep purple-black aubergines flaunted their pristine, shiny skin. Vegetables were harvested, whole spices were toasted and the heady aroma of freshly diced ingredients would fill the humid air and draw hunger from the pit of my dad's belly. These unfussy meals would be served with stacks of blistered rotis slapped with butter that dripped through fingers and into the bowls of vibrant vegetarian curry.

Big fat tomatoes, the juicy kind which my father would often gobble as a piece of fruit in Karachi, weren't as readily available at the International Store in Cambridge in 1962. So he improvised with a tin of chopped tomatoes, combined them with *exotic* Spanish onions and a basket of potatoes, and threw in a friendly dose of spices to remind him of what his body missed so much. The result, a salivating piece of culinary minimalism with some of the cheapest ingredients money can buy.

ALOO TIMATER

Serves 4 as a side or 2 as a main

3 medium onions
3 tbsp corn oil
1 tsp panch puran (see box)
700g red-skinned waxy potatoes, peeled and chopped into
   bite-size chunks
2–3 green chillies, sliced
Salt
125ml water
1 x 400g tin of tomatoes
Handful of fresh coriander leaves, to serve

The trick with this dish is to keep it simple. It's a quick, tasty recipe which comes to life with the bouquet of spices. Chop the onions into cubes and fry in the oil in a lidded frying pan until translucent. Pitch in the panch puran and coat the onion chunks. Add the potatoes, slip in the chillies, give it a little salt and tip in the water. The pan will sizzle and throw up a blissful scent of the spice mix. Turn the heat down, put the lid on and let the spuds cook until they're 90 per cent done. Check by piercing a fork into a potato piece. It should slide in easily without breaking apart. Pop in the tomatoes, turn the heat up and cook for a further 5 minutes or until the edges of the potatoes blur. Stir regularly but allow the tomatoes to retain a rough chunky texture. Add a little water if it becomes too dry and starts to stick. Dress with fresh coriander leaves.

    Serve as a side dish or as a main with a flat bread of choice.

PANCH PURAN

This is a heady 5-spice mix of pan-fried whole spice which can be recklessly bashed into a fine powder or left whole and then added to deliver an intensity to curry recipes, especially veggie ones. Take equal amounts of each of the following;

Cumin seeds
Coriander seeds
Fennel seeds
Fenugreek
Kalonji (nigella) seeds

Heat a frying pan on medium and throw in all the ingredients. Gently move them around until they brown and start to perfume the pan. Take them off the heat and let them cool, then pop them in a mortar and beat them with a pestle until transformed into a light fluffy mound of aromatic bliss.

VICTOR'S FINISHING TOUCH

Just as a debutante's tiara finishes off a look, chutneys and pickles add grace to most Indian subcontinent recipes. Depending on the occasion, they lend a refreshing, fiery, textural, sharp or piquant component to meals. Sitting patiently on the side waiting to be spooned, dunked, dipped, or drizzled on to recipes, they're the perfect wing man to the main affair. This is my father Victor's recipe, affectionately known as Vicki Chutney. I prefer it a little runnier than usual as it's easier to ladle on to recipes such as Daal Chawal (page 64). It's easier than breathing and quicker than a shooting star.

VICKI CHUTNEY

Makes enough for over 10 servings

Half an onion, peeled
1 tomato
2 tsp tamarind concentrate
1 green chilli
2cm fresh root ginger, peeled
   and finely chopped

1 garlic clove
Handful of fresh mint and
   coriander leaves
1 tbsp flaked coconut
50ml water
Juice of half a lemon
Salt to taste

Now the hard part. Throw it all into a blender and blitz. The result will be a sharp, fresh-scented chutney, perfect for rice dishes and kebabs.

VICTOR'S WEDDING FEAST

Asian weddings are loud, bold, fat, dazzling and long.

Saris shine like bright boiled sweet wrappers, adorned with magnificent gold stitching. Feet and hands are finely dyed with ancient henna designs, and gold jewellery gleams with an intensity unlike any other. The result is a glittering symphony of colour, sound and smell. These weddings grab the senses in every way. The dancing is euphoric and relentless, the music will leave your eardrums begging for mercy, and the food … well, it's not called a wedding feast for nothing.

My cousin Terry's wedding was no exception. He got hitched in Karachi and they celebrated BIG style. No expense was spared, and naturally the food was the central pillar of the party. It had been years since Dad had visited Pakistan and he'd missed the taste of indigenous curry. This recipe is one of the most delectable he's passed on. It's one that was used to rejoice in my cousin's happiness, and as a result I cook it when I want to create something special. It's perfect for a dinner party with great mates, or a family gathering. Prepare it a day in advance if you can (meat-based curries always taste better a day later). Cook more than you need and freeze the leftovers.

This style of cooking meat comes from the south-east Sindh province in Pakistan and is cooked *bughela*-style (pronounced 'boo-gay-la'). This process uses boiling water, ensuring that the meat takes on a tender texture. The province takes its name from the original Sindhus river, now known as the Indus, and it may have been this connection with water that inspired this method. The beef is tender and falling apart, and if you listen carefully you'll hear an Asian wedding party in full swing.

BEEF BUGHELA

Serves 4 and then some

1kg stewing beef, chopped
2 medium onions, finely sliced
3 garlic cloves, chopped
3 green chillies, chopped
5cm fresh root ginger, peeled and sliced into matchsticks
1 tsp ground garam masala (see page 46)
2 tbsp medium curry powder
1 tsp ground coriander
2 tbsp whole garam masala (2 tsp cumin seeds, 1 tsp cloves,
    2 tsp teaspoon whole coriander seeds, 1 tsp whole pepper)
2 tbsp sunflower oil
500g natural yoghurt, fork whipped and at room temperature
    (I like to use one with 10% fat but you can use a low-fat
    yoghurt if preferred)
Big scooped handful of fresh chopped coriander

This method of cooking relies on the balance of water and spice. It's an unusual way of measuring water quantities but as pot sizes vary it's best to follow this traditional technique.

Put the beef in a large pot and mark out 5cm above the height of the beef. Remove the beef and fill the pot with salted water up to the measured point. Bring the water to the boil and add the beef (really important – do not brown it or you'll screw the dish up). Continue boiling on a medium heat until all the yucky foam reaches the surface, scooping it off with a slotted spoon until the water is clear, then boil for a further 30 minutes. Throughout the process, leave the pot uncovered – you're looking to produce an intense, reduced sauce.

Slide in the onions, garlic, chilli and ginger and cook for 30 minutes on a low heat; the water will reduce a little.

Gently stir. Add the ground garam masala, curry powder and ground coriander and cook for a further 30 minutes. It takes a while but stick with it.

Drop in the whole garam masala and cook for 20 minutes, then incrementally add the yoghurt tablespoon by tablespoon, stirring gently each time, making sure it's assimilated and doesn't curdle and get gritty. Keep stirring, then add a glug of oil until it rises to the top and the curry looks silky. The beef should be tender and almost flaky. Lastly, add the chopped coriander and stir in. It'll finish off the curry beautifully.

Eat with piping hot Chapattis (page 172).

GROUND GARAM MASALA

Ground *garam* (Hindi for hot) *masala* (paste) is a staple combination used in the vast majority of subcontinent curries. It's pungent, necessary and it's easy to make. This is the most essential form of the mixture.

¼ tsp cumin seeds
½ tsp coriander seeds
½ tsp black peppercorns
2 green cardamom pods
4 cloves
¼ tsp ground mace

Heat a frying pan on a medium heat and pop in all the ingredients except the ground mace. Dry-roast the spices for 2 minutes until they jig and hop in the pan, taking care not to burn them. They will volunteer an aroma which is hard to forget. Leave to cool, peel the cardamom pods and release the seeds into the other spices, add the mace and tip into a pestle and mortar (or blender) and punish them until they yield into fluffy powder. Surplus can be kept in an airtight container, though it will degrade and lose its bouquet over time.

GRANDSTAND MEATBALLS

Like relationships, sometimes it takes a while for recipes and cooking flair to mature.

Divorce in the 1970s wasn't so common, and even less so in Asian circles. For me as a kid it was like having six fingers on one hand: most of the time you fitted in but every now and then someone noticed you were different (but what an advantage for playing the recorder). Estranged from my mother but living just down the road, my father would spend weekends with me and my brother, and this always included a bout of sport, either watching or playing it. We would kick a football around the park, using jumpers for goal posts, or watch our local Indian football team, Punjab United, train. It seemed you could only play for them if you had the surname Patel.

As we caught the late Saturday afternoon football results on BBC1's *Grandstand*, the mood in my father's two-up two-down rental rose or fell according to Leeds United's performance. It was during this period of anticipation that Dad would get to work in the tiny kitchen, toasting spices, grinding his masala, simmering sauces and cupping his oiled hands to shape walnut-sized lamb meatballs (kofte). He'd peer round the kitchen door to catch the latest results and commandeer an extra pair of hands to chop coriander. Our family team's performance was largely inconsistent, as was this recipe in its earlier days. Sometimes the gravy was a little too thin or the onions not soft enough, but time has a habit of improving things to a state of maturity, as it did with our relationship. This dish has flourished into something altogether richer, complete and happy. I just wish our football team had followed suit.

LAMB KOFTE

Serves up to 6

500g minced lamb
1 tsp crushed garlic
1 large onion, finely chopped
4 green finger chillies, finely chopped
1 tsp salt
1 egg, fork-whisked
4 tbsp oil

Pop all the ingredients except the oil in a large bowl, squishing everything together. Wash your hands and rub a little oil over your palms. Grab a walnut-sized piece of the mixture and shape it into a ball. You should end up with 20–24 meatballs.

Heat the oil in a frying pan, add the meatballs in batches, browning them all over, take them out with a slotted spoon and place on kitchen paper.

BLACK CARDAMOM CURRY SAUCE

Serves up to 6

2 tbsp vegetable oil
1 tsp cumin seeds
1 large onion, finely sliced
4 black cardamom pods
2cm fresh root ginger, peeled and finely chopped
2 garlic cloves, crushed
400g chopped tinned tomatoes
2 tbsp tomato purée
1 tsp salt (more if you prefer)
1 tsp turmeric powder
1 tsp chilli powder
1 tsp garam masala (see page 46)
Lamb Kofte (see opposite)
Fresh coriander leaves, chopped, to garnish

Take a large pan and warm the oil over a medium heat until hot, then add the cumin seeds and fry for about a minute until aromatic. Drop in the onions and fry until soft and translucent, then introduce the cardamom, ginger and garlic and fry for a minute. Pop in the tomatoes and the purée, season with salt, then add the turmeric, chilli powder and garam masala and cook for a further 10 minutes until the oil rises to the surface, giving the curry a soft sheen. Add the kofta meatballs and simmer for 20 minutes. For best results cook the night before eating. Garnish with chopped coriander.

Serve with fluffy basmati rice or flatbreads and Desi Salad (see page 181).

THE AMERICAN DREAM

The sea air was thick with the smell of salt, fish and the hum of hard graft. As a child, Dad would swing his feet from the harbour wall and watch the fisherman's skinny cinnamon arms and legs haul in their nets and pull their paint blistered vessels into port. The big open sky and the thought of a land beyond these shores mystified him, but it was the scent of fresh fish and prawns in particular that set his head swaying in the breeze. Karachi's position by the ocean meant that the family would tuck into a fish or prawn supper at least once a week. The pink prawns would sit in a pool of crimson gravy, and little Victor along with his brothers and sisters would await the starter's orders. In this case it would be Dhadha-ji saying grace and then the trap doors to their jaws would drop and the race to taste the sharp, sour yet sweet tang on their tongues began.

In the mid-1980s and in his early forties, Dad found himself far from Karachi's coastline and in the New World of California, America. Aching from the separation of his family and his now ex-wife, he resolved to begin a new life away from the constant reminder of a family he was no longer actively part of. It had been more than twenty years since he emigrated to England and the prospect of starting again filled him with a sense of fear and adventure. Embracing the American dream dominated his every waking moment, and he decided the best way into people's hearts was via their tummies. He hosted successive dinner parties and grew his network of friends and business connections. He refined his cooking methods, learnt new dishes and seduced them with recipes from old. Jhinga Masala ('prawn tang') is a temptress and will lead you on, begging for more of her silky red allure, beyond the point of no return.

JHINGA MASALA

Serves 4 and a bit more (keep some for yourself)

750g medium prawns, peeled and cooked
¼ tsp turmeric, then another ¼ tsp
¼ tsp chilli powder
2 medium white onions
6 medium tomatoes
4 garlic cloves, peeled
5cm fresh root ginger, peeled and chopped
3 green chillies
2 tbsp Madras curry powder
250ml water
Salt
3 tbsp sunflower oil
½ tsp black mustard seeds
1 tbsp malt vinegar
2 tsp coconut powder
½ tsp sugar
2 tsp ground garam masala (see page 53)
A big handful of coriander leaves
Half a lemon
Curry leaves (optional), to finish

The key thing with this dish is not to overcook the prawns, particularly if you're using pre-cooked ones. Coat them in ¼ tsp turmeric and the chilli powder, cover and refrigerate for at least one hour. Chop both onions into quarters and put one quarter aside. Pop the rest in a blender along with the tomatoes, garlic, ginger, chillies, curry powder, the other ¼ tsp turmeric, water and generous pinch of salt.

Heat the oil in a largish pan on a medium setting and sprinkle in the mustard seeds. Wait for them to hop around

and then add the remaining sliced onion and let it soften. Drop in the blended ingredients with the vinegar, coconut powder and sugar and boil for 10 minutes on a low heat. Keep the gravy runny, with a silken consistency rather than watery. As the surface of the curry glistens with the rising oil, add the freshly ground garam masala and stir until assimilated. Be patient, and let it boil for another 8 minutes. Introduce the prawns to the pan and let them cook for 5 minutes (10 minutes if using uncooked peeled prawns), adding the coriander leaves and a squeeze of lemon before serving. To dress the dish you could always fry some curry leaves until crispy in a separate pan and sprinkle on top.

This is a runny dish, so best served with rice or armfuls of puffy naans.

FRAGRANT GARAM MASALA

The scent of this garam masala combines perfectly with the subtlety of prawns. It won't overpower it, but it will add accents that beautifully accessorise this dish.

1 tsp fennel seeds
½ tsp cumin seeds
1 tsp coriander seeds
1 tsp black peppercorns
½ tsp cardamom seeds (from 4–5 green pods)
4 cloves
4 star anise
2 x 2cm cinnamon quills

Heat a frying pan on a medium heat and add in all the ingredients. Dry-roast the spices for 2 minutes until they brown and start to scent the room. DON'T burn them. Leave to cool, peel the cardamom pods and release the seeds into the other spices, tip into a pestle and mortar (or blender) and blast them.

UNCLE SAM'S QUICK VEGETABLE CURRIES

'Welcome to the land of the free and home of the brave.'

It's a mantra my father has repeated throughout his twenty-five-plus years in the USA. He identifies this as possibly the freest he's ever felt, and at the time of his migration he summoned bravery he hoped would carry him to his dreams. His vision of a comfortable life was met with the familiar face of hard graft. He often juggled jobs, working in a gas station, dabbling in financial services, operating concessions, and he had a portfolio career consisting of long hours with little time during the week to cook gourmet curry. Quick-fire recipes consisted of vegetarian dishes that he could eat between jobs and conserve for later. He blended spices from the East with a Californian zeal for healthy eating and well-being. Haste is a key ingredient in these short-on-time recipes that refuse to compromise on taste and texture.

FRISCO ZUCCHINI

Serves 4 as a side to Stolen Chicken (page 144)
or 2 as a main

Olive oil (preferably extra virgin)
1 tsp black mustard seeds
½ tsp cumin seeds
⅓ tsp fennel seeds
Half an onion, sliced
1 garlic clove, sliced
2 courgettes, chopped into thick batons (2cm thick x 6cm long)
1.5cm fresh root ginger, peeled and sliced
Asafoetida, pinch
Salt and pepper

Splash a little oil into a frying pan over a medium to high heat and drop in the mustard seeds. Allow them to fizz and pop, then add the cumin and fennel seeds and push them around the pan for 30 seconds or so until they give in and submit their scent. Introduce the sliced onion and combine all the ingredients until the onion is coated in the whole spices and turning a buttery colour. Pop in the garlic and ginger, stirring for about a minute. Add the courgettes and cook for 2–3 minutes, stirring until they're all over each other, season with a touch of salt and pepper. Now it's time to pitch in a pinch of asafoetida (which stinks at first but amazingly becomes mellow and smooth). Cook for a further 10–12 minutes until the courgettes have become tender but not soggy. Serve hot straight from the pan.

BAYSIDE BAINGAN

Serves 4 as a side to Aloo Timater (page 40)
or Passanda (page 100) or 2 as a main

2 fat aubergines	Pinch of salt
1 onion, sliced	½ tsp sugar
3 tbsp vegetable oil	Panch puran (see page 41;
½ tsp turmeric powder	optional)
½ tsp chilli powder	Half a lemon
250ml chopped tinned	
tomatoes	

This dish takes advantage of the aubergine's vulnerability, and they will end up nicely crushed. First dice the aubergines. Fry the onion in the oil in a largish pan on a low to medium heat until soft and brown. Add the aubergines and cook until they're soft and have yielded a little moisture. With the back of a cooking spoon (I use a wooden one), crush these little baingan cubes until they've splayed out a little. Now add the turmeric, chilli powder, tomatoes, salt, sugar (and panch puran, if using). Mix it up thoroughly. After 15 minutes, the edges of the pan should be sizzling a little with the activity of the ingredients and starting to crackle. Keep stirring, and taste a little, seasoning further if required. Just before serving, add the juice of half a lemon. It's ready; what are you waiting for?

GOVERNOR VIC'S GHOBI

*Serves 4 as a side to fish or Mama Peters' Jhalfrezi
(page 18) or 2 as a main*

1 large cauliflower
3 tbsp vegetable oil
1 onion, sliced
1 tsp mustard seeds
1 tsp cumin seeds
Pinch of salt
½ tsp turmeric powder
½ tsp chilli powder
200ml chopped tinned tomatoes

Chop the cauliflower into bite-size florets. In a large frying pan, warm the vegetable oil and cook the onion on a medium heat until golden brown. Add mustard seeds and cumin seeds and wait for them to pop and sizzle. Quickly add the cauliflower and stir vigorously, ensuring the spices coat everything. After 5 minutes, introduce the salt, turmeric, chilli powder and tomatoes, cooking for a further 10 minutes. The tomatoes should be clinging to the cauliflower like best friends, with the pan starting to sound as if it's drying out a little and crackling. Now's the time to take it off the heat and serve whilst hot.

CALIFORNIA CABBAGE SIZZLE

Serves 4 as a side to Shift Chicken Curry (page 117)
or 2 as a main

1 large white cabbage, finely sliced into shards
3 tbsp vegetable oil
1 tsp fennel seeds
1 tsp mustard seeds
1 tsp cumin seeds
1 onion, sliced
6cm fresh root ginger, peeled and chopped
2 green chillies, chopped
3 large tomatoes, diced
Pinch of salt

This is a super-quick dish. Finely slice the white cabbage into shards. Over a medium heat, warm the oil in a large frying pan and tip in all the seeds. As soon as they do their customary dance, slide in the onion and ginger. Stir all the ingredients and cook for further 3–5 minutes or until the onions have tanned and the ginger is slightly crispy. Now add the cabbage and chillies. Agitate everything and cook for 5 minutes until the cabbage has softened, then introduce the tomatoes and salt. Whack the heat down to low and let the ingredients do their work for approximately 8–10 minutes. As the tomatoes blend with the rest of their friends, you'll see them starting to sizzle and dry a little. It's ready to be served straight from the pan.

* super quick dish!

California Cabbage Sizzle
(serves 4 as a side or 2 as a main)
1 large white cabbage, finely sliced
into shards

ALOO AND MOTI MIRCH

Serves 4 as a side dish to Lawrie's Lamb Bhuna (page 222) or 2 as a main

4 medium sized potatoes
4 peppers a mix of green, yellow and red
2 onions, finely sliced
4 tbsp olive oil
½ tsp sugar
1 tsp mustard seeds
1 tsp cumin seeds
½ tsp turmeric powder
2 fresh green chillies, chopped (or ½ tsp chilli powder)
200g tinned chopped tomatoes
Salt
Juice of half a lemon

Peel the potatoes and chop into small chunks. Slice the peppers into six pieces, lengthways. Fry half the onion rings in half the oil in a frying pan over medium to high heat. When beginning to brown, add a little sugar to caramelise them, and when gorgeously brown remove to add later. In the same pan over a medium heat, add another glug of oil and fry the mustard and cumin seeds until they pop, then add the remaining onions and cook until translucent. Add the potatoes, turmeric and chillies, cooking for about 10 minutes or until the spuds have softened around the edges. Now's the time for the peppers and tomatoes to step in; throw them in with a dash of salt. Simmer for around 10–15 minutes or until the peppers have yielded, and the potatoes are cooked through and coated with sticky tomatoes. Anoint with lemon juice and serve piping hot.

ALOO KI BURTHA

***Serves 4 as a side to Kofte Curry (page 49) or to stuff
Parathas (page 37)***

450g floury potatoes, boiled and peeled
1 medium onion, diced finely
3 tbsp olive oil
½ tsp cumin seeds
2 green chillies, chopped
½ tsp turmeric
⅓ tsp chilli powder
2 large tomatoes, deseeded and finely chopped
1 tsp salt
Fist of coriander leaves, chopped
100g unsalted butter (optional)

Mash the boiled potatoes coarsely. Fry the onion in the oil
in a large pan until opaque and still retaining a little crunch.
Add the cumin seeds, chillies, turmeric and chilli powder,
stirring until the mix has dried a little and is starting to
scent the pan. Add this masala to the potatoes and combine
thoroughly together with the freshly chopped tomatoes, salt
and coriander. The burtha should take on a sunny disposition as the turmeric colours its complexion. If you're looking
for a smoother taste, mix in the butter, but the consistency
should remain rough rather than puréed. Gloriously simple
and deliciously cheap, you could use it as an alternative to
mash.

CAMPING CHAWAL

Having sworn his allegiance to the flag, my father proudly counted himself as part of America's adopted family. His language switched to American English in a flash. Petrol was now gas, tramps were bums, rubbish was trash and everything was bigger. Keen to explore his new-found home on the West Coast, he packed an SUV with enough camping equipment and stocks to organise a military manoeuvre and feed a platoon. In went the tent, stove, ground mats, and together with some of his extended family, who had also made the journey from Pakistan to live in the US – Aggie (his niece), her husband and their children – there was enough excess baggage to keep Pan Am still in business. As they blasted down CA-1 along the twisty Californian Highway, travelling south through Monterey County to Carmel and on to Pebble Beach, their Bollywood sing-along was interrupted by snapshots of rugged beauty: cliffs dramatically falling into the Pacific, the dense scent of pine, impressive kelp forests, tide pools gurgling below the highway and sea lions yawning on their rocky perches. Every curve and turn framed a view of unstoppable beauty.

For most adults, camping conjures images of soggy socks, water rationing, a poor night's sleep and an idea of what to inflict on your children in future years. For my family, canvas living was a novelty, an adventure waiting to be unveiled.

After two hours of tent erection, they flung out the floral orange bedspread on their camping pitch high atop the cliffs of Big Sur, a view filled with a modern interpretation of a Turner painting. The sky, injected with pink, yellow and purple ink, smiled down on the undulating curves of the Pacific. With the campers grumbling for food, the gas stove was fired up and containers of food were cracked open, releasing the aroma of Asian 'camp food'. Bright yellow daal was flecked with soft white grains of rice (daal chawal) and punctuated with whole spices. Carefully wrapped parathas were passed around and teeth were sunk into juicy tandoori lamb chops, whilst spoonfuls of refreshing mint and coriander chutney balanced the menu. No barbecued burgers or bangers here, just the scent and taste of simple home-cooked food, remixed in California. As they sat crossed-legged and filling their bellies with sustenance, Dad ran his tongue across his teeth, smacking his lips together with delight and said what they were all thinking. 'You can take the boy out of Pakistan, but you can't take Pakistan out of the boy.'

DAAL CHAWAL

Serves up to 6

250g moong daal (bright yellow lentils)
350ml water
2 tomatoes, chopped, retaining seeds
1 tsp turmeric powder
2 green chillies, chopped
3cm fresh root ginger, peeled and finely chopped
Salt
400g basmati rice
2 bay leaves
1 cinnamon quill
Tadka (see box)
2 tbsp oil

Soak the daal for 30 minutes, then drain and rinse well.

Over a medium heat, boil the water and add the daal, tomatoes, turmeric, chillies, ginger, oil and ½ tsp salt, cooking for approximately 35 minutes. The daal should keep its shape and not turn too mushy.

As the daal is cooking, in a separate pot boil the rice, bay leaves, cinnamon quill and a pinch of salt. Cook for around 20 minutes or until it's almost done, i.e. still a touch firm. Once ready, drain and pop it back in the pan.

Now it's time to make the tadka (see the box), which when mixed into the daal gives it a real kick of intense flavours.

Layer the daal over the rice in the pot, add 80ml water, cover and let everything steam for about 5 minutes. Take off the heat and mix up the daal and rice, and serve hot with a side of Vicki Chutney (see page 42).

Daal chawal keeps well in the fridge. It's easy to reheat and can be devoured later.

VP'S SIMPLE TADKA — NO. 2

This is the same approach my father uses for his Palak Saag (see page 16). It's super-quick and it's a total flavour enhancer.

2 tbsp olive oil
1 large onion, finely sliced
2 garlic cloves, chopped
5cm fresh root ginger, peeled and chopped
1 long green chilli
½ tsp brown mustard seeds
Salt and pepper

Warm a frying pan on a medium heat and add the oil. When hot, pop in the onion and garlic, allowing them to brown and crisp at the edges. Add the ginger, chilli and mustard seeds and turn up the heat a little, until the seeds jig and hop in the pan. Fry for a further 3–4 minutes until the ginger has softened and the chilli has turned from green to a dullish brown, season with salt and pepper, then take off the heat and leave to cool.

VICKI-CHACHU'S LADIES' FINGERS

Pet names abound in Asian families. Often they take the place of a birth name. Florence, my mother, has the nickname Papu; I have a cousin aptly referred to as Bubbly (christened Marian); I have an aunt called Gillo (Gloria), another known as Cullay (Lorena), and my dad is known to my cousins as Vicki-Chachu ('chachu' quite properly refers to my father as their dad's younger brother, and Vicki is adapted from 'Victor'). It's a tradition which is warmly received and exchanged by each generation. The names are affectionate and commonly used when asking for something, almost like a 'pretty please'. However, with our family the requests are rarely about something material. If you can cook it, taste it, savour it, chew it and swallow it, then it will find a way into our hearts. Such is the case with my dad's okra recipe, or bhindi, as it's known across the subcontinent, and, rather elegantly, 'ladies' fingers', as it's referred to by many others.

Whilst living in the USA and eating more vegetables than ever before to balance his meat intake, he perfected this recipe. Using slim okra, he transforms them into juicy, ginger-flashed digits of vibrant green, slashed with red and gold as the tomatoes, garlic and onions go to work. The

pan takes on the palette of a sari shop, whilst the scent is earthy, yet clean and light. No wonder the chorus goes up whenever Dad's in town. 'Vicki-Chachu, can you cook us ladies' fingers?' Perfect with fish or seafood dishes.

LADIES' FINGERS

Serves 4 as a side or 2 as a main

4 tbsp olive oil
1 tsp black mustard seeds
½ tsp cumin seeds
2 medium onions, finely chopped
3 garlic cloves, finely chopped
2 green chillies, chopped
1 tsp ground coriander
7.5cm fresh root ginger, peeled and cut into fine matchsticks
400g okra, washed, dried, topped and tailed
2 fat tomatoes, chopped, retaining seeds and skin
Salt and pepper

This spiced okra is so straightforward it's laughable. Over a medium heat, warm the oil and then pop in the mustard seeds. When they pop, add the cumin seeds for a minute, then slide in the onions and garlic. Let the onions soften until opaque, then drop in the chillies and ground coriander, and stir for a couple of minutes, coating everything with everything. Now add the ginger and push around the pan vigorously. The aroma will assault you, and when it does, it's time to introduce the okra. Like ladies' fingers, they're delicate and need to be treated with care. So gently push them around the pan for around 2 minutes until they turn a deeper shade of green, then add the tomatoes for sharpness, season with salt and pepper and cook over a high heat for a further 5–6 minutes. The bhindi should feel on the verge of al dente, but not stringy.

Tuck in with a Chapatti or two (page 172).

PUKKA PAKORAS

'"*Achar, Victor, bawth pukka hé*" – that's the rating they gave my pakoras last Saturday.' (Loosely translated as, 'These are awesome.')

I could tell Dad was beaming when I spoke to him on a long-distance Californian phone call as he detailed the menu for a recent soirée at his house. A septuagenarian who still loves to party – I've inherited a great set of genes. He ran through the dishes and critiqued each one, adjusting spice quantities to refine his recipes for his next shindig. His parties know no age boundaries; they are a mix of senior wisdom, youthful energy and middle-age reflection. He's gathered friends like a young boy collects marbles: each special, different and carrying a signature to their character.

'The star of the show was definitely the pakoras. They are getting better each time I make them. You *need* to try them out.'

I remember facing heaps of pakoras at an early age, the batter-fried vegetable fritters sitting like an Everest challenge to all the guests at our family's frequent parties. Tables quivered under their weight. We grazed on the ridges of the pakora mountain, gradually depleting it to crumbs. Dipping misshapen, crispy blobs of spiced batter into sweet chutney, and crunching through the surface of the pakora into the vaguely concealed vegetable beneath, we knew it was party time.

For my father, the party's still going on, and I've got a feeling we'll be eating his pukka pakoras even when the party's stopped.

PAKORAS

Serves 4 or more

250g gram (chickpea) flour
50g baking powder
3 green chillies, finely chopped
1 large onion, finely sliced
½ tsp chilli powder
2 tbsp freshly chopped coriander leaves
Salt
100ml vegetable oil, for frying
400g large fresh spinach leaves, washed, stems trimmed
    but not cut off

Pop the flour, baking powder, chillies, onion, chilli powder and coriander into a large bowl, seasoning with a touch of salt, and mix in enough water to make a thick, sticky batter. My advice is that this is intuitive, and you're best ladling in tablespoons of water at a time until it's of a consistency to coat a spinach leaf easily. The batter shouldn't be too drippy.

In a deep frying pan or wok, heat the oil until hot. Test it by dropping in a small blob of batter. It should turn golden in less than a minute. In batches, dip the large spinach leaves into the coating and gently lower them into the oil, cooking them until bronzed, for around 3 minutes. Remove with a slotted spoon and drain on paper towel. Eat hot, straight away, with a sweet chilli dipping chutney.

Alternatively, you can use a variety of pre-cooked al dente vegetables to dip in the batter, such as broccoli, cauliflower, courgette and carrot.

GUDDU CHACHU

(UNCLE STANLEY)

GUDDU CHACHU

Stanley Peters, aka Guddu Chachu, wore the look of a Pakistani fast bowler: lithe, springy and alert.

My earliest memory of Guddu Chachu is of a tall slim man with cinnamon skin and a Sweeney-style 1970s moustache. Being the youngest of seven, he was carefree and spirited, blessed with greater freedom and affection than his siblings, and he was often regarded as the darling of the family. His best friend was made of willow and was by his side constantly. As he struck deft blows to home-fashioned cricket balls into the Karachi sun, he adopted selective deafness, often ignoring his mother's calls to come in for dinner. His twinkly eyes, boyish charm and cheeky wit would lead either to favour or to fisticuffs in the Drigh Road estate in Karachi, both of which he embraced with gusto. His competitive edge pushed him academically and athletically as he studied economics in his hometown at St Patrick's College and spent every possible moment practising his bowling and batting techniques. He dreamt of glory, and of striding from the pavilion decked in his whites to the roar of fans at the National Stadium. His aspiration was almost in reach as he trialled at the fertile recruitment ground of the Karachi Cricket Club, from which Test Match cricketers are cultivated. However, at an early age he discovered the acerbic tang of discrimination. He had the talent but not the status of richer, middle-class families,

whose connections assured a place in the batting line-up. The words of the adored Pakistani Test Match cricket hero Wallis Matthias still ring painfully in Guddu Chachu's ears: 'If it was up to me, you'd be selected, but your family doesn't have the social credentials.' He knew then that life would be full of graft, but he was determined to get the most out of it.

Like his older brothers and sisters, his field of dreams lay outside the Pakistani home into which he was born in 1948, shortly after the biggest upheaval in the subcontinent's history, which brought partition and the birth of Pakistani independence.

Although finances were always tight in such a large family, being the youngest had its benefits. By now his older brothers and sisters were all working and pitching into the family coffers, making life a little sweeter for Guddu Chachu. The family friend 'frugal' had outstayed his welcome and Pakistan wasn't quite swinging in the 1960s, so one by one his siblings, together with their mother, sought fortune in foreign climes: the land of promise … England. This temporary separation, whilst heartbreaking, was commonplace for migrating families. The exodus left Guddu Chachu and his father (Dhadha-ji) to fend for themselves. Staring at each other across a sparse dining table, his father dispatched the order, 'I'll cook, you clean.' He wasn't fond of Marigold gloves, so two years later Guddu Chachu was in England too. He began his cooking innings in Blighty and he's still yet to declare.

COMFORT DAAL

Working up to his final century, Guddu Chachu would stir from his cricketing somnambulism, realising that the roar from the imaginary Karachi crowd was in fact his mother yelling his name with disciplinary warning. If he didn't join the family dining table in less than a minute, his cricket bat would be re-employed to strike a new target. Sulkily proclaiming his personal best, he joined his older siblings. The air was filled with the sweet smell of caramelised onions, toasted garlic and the infantry charge of chilli – the unmistakable aroma of tadka daal. Although he associates it with the smell of autumn and street hawkers roasting monkey nuts or frying river fish such as palla, the truth is they consumed this lentil dish all year round. But Guddu Chachu best enjoyed the warmth of daal in the cooler months. The sweet-sour taste of yellow lentils mixed with pan-fried whole spice saturated him with a feeling of comfort and home, and even now in his greying years he refers to this dish as 'comfort daal', perhaps because it doesn't involve cutlery. It's sweet, it's sour, it's the taste of every family and it will caress you with well-being.

TADKA DAAL

Serves 4

120g red split lentils
60g moong daal (yellow ones)
600ml water
2 garlic cloves, chopped
   roughly

½ tsp turmeric powder
2 green chillies, chopped
¼ tsp sugar
1 lemon

Soak both types of lentils for 15 minutes, then drain and rinse. Put in a pan with the water and bring to the boil. Add the garlic, turmeric, chillies and sugar, cooking for 25–30 minutes until the lentils have lost their shape and look mushy. Add

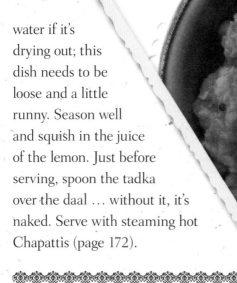

water if it's drying out; this dish needs to be loose and a little runny. Season well and squish in the juice of the lemon. Just before serving, spoon the tadka over the daal … without it, it's naked. Serve with steaming hot Chapattis (page 172).

STAN'S TADKA

2 tbsp vegetable oil
1 onion, sliced
2 garlic cloves, roughly chopped
2cm fresh root ginger, peeled
3 dried red chillies
½ tsp mustard seeds
½ tsp black onion seeds, sometimes referred to as Kalonji or Nigella seeds
½ tsp cumin seeds
1 tomato, diced
Salt and pepper

Warm a frying pan on a medium heat and add the oil. When hot, pop in the onion and garlic, allowing them to brown and crisp at the edges. Add the ginger, chillies and all the seeds, then turn up the heat until the seeds jig and hop in the pan. Add the tomato, frying for a further 3–4 minutes until the ginger has softened and the tadka has dried a little. Season, take off the heat, cover immediately to retain the spice hit and leave to cool.

STREET FOOD

'Watch out for trains. And don't spill any!'

The water slapped the sides of the pail and the yoke across Guddu Chachu's shoulders gnawed at his muscles, sweat crowning his brow. He passed a hot palm across his forehead and paused before crossing the busy train track, allowing passenger-choked carriages to whistle by. Setting down the family household water, he contemplated the two-mile hike back home, dodging rickshaws, squinting at the sun's orange ferocity, whilst his nostrils fought the dust of the roads. This was hard work for an eight-year-old, but a necessary family chore for a household without running water. His daydreams would carry him home and, as he neared the house, his eyes brightened and his taste buds thickened. It was always the alluring smell of street food that distracted him from his straining pain, with the possibility of a family treat at Café George. The Iranian owners served the city's best lamb pastries – spiced mince wrapped in flaky pastry. His nose would lead him to street hawkers dishing fiery fried chillies, aloo tikki (scrummy potato cutlets), samosas and pani puri. He'd slake his thirst with lemonade as fresh as starlight and his joy would be complete. His job as pani wallah (water boy) was sweetened by simple pleasures: food served straight from the streets of Karachi. He loved it, and you'll want to devour it.

ALOO TIKKI

Serves up to 6 as starter, snack or party food

500g potatoes, boiled and peeled
1 mild onion, finely chopped
75g green peas, boiled
3 chillies (2 green and 1 red), chopped
fistful of coriander leaves, chopped
2.5cm fresh root ginger, peeled and finely chopped
1 tsp cumin seeds, roasted and bashed into powder
juice of ½ lemon
1 egg, fork-whisked
Salt and pepper
Flour, for dusting
Vegetable oil, enough for shallow-frying (around 5mm depth
in a frying pan)

Pop all the ingredients (not the oil or flour) into a bowl and mash, keeping the ingredients coarse. Divide into 10–12 portions. Squish them into thick flat tikkis (which translates as 'cutlets') with the palm of your hand, then coat them in flour. Cool in a fridge for 30 minutes to firm them up.

Heat oil in a large frying pan over a medium heat, then fry the aloo tikki until crisp and golden brown on both sides. Serve hot with Sweet and Sour Tomato Chutney (page 87).

GREEN FRIED CHILLIES

Serves 6 as a snack

1 tbsp coriander seeds	1 tsp brown sugar
1 tsp cumin seeds	1 tbsp garlic paste
2 tbsp sesame seeds	(see page 93)
1 tsp poppy seeds	1 tbsp ginger paste
3 tbsp cashew nuts	(see page 93)
1 tbsp grated or desiccated	1 tsp ground coriander
coconut	½ tsp turmeric powder
1 onion, roughly chopped	Salt

For the frying pan
6–8 fat green chillies, split on one side and deseeded
150ml vegetable oil

This might seem like a lot of bother for such diddy little spice pistols, but this piquant snack is well worth the time, and so evocative of the busy Indian streets it comes from.

Roast the seeds, nuts and coconut in a frying pan for 3 minutes, until they yield their scent. Leave to cool. Tip these roasted spices, along with the onion, sugar, pastes, coriander and turmeric into a blender and pulse into a smooth paste. Season with salt. Stuff the split chillies with the paste.

In a large deep frying pan or wok, heat the oil over a medium setting, slip in the stuffed chillies and any extra stuffing paste, and fry until the chillies have taken on a brown, blistered appearance: about 5–8 minutes. Remove and drain on kitchen paper.

Serve with a rinsing of lime juice.

CAFÉ GEORGE'S SPECIALITY

For me these have almost achieved the status of beatification. They are without doubt one of Guddu Chachu's defining culinary accomplishments. Flaky glazed pastry envelopes of highly charged mince, soaking up just enough of the spiced juices and finely chopped chillies to leave the palate with a delicate tingle. They're great for a houseful of dinner guests, or delicious for a party of one.

LAMB PASTRIES

Makes 14–16

500g lamb mince
4–6 green chillies, finely chopped (quantity depends
    on your heat resistance)
1 onion, finely diced
1 tsp salt
⅓ tsp garam masala (see page 46)
½ tsp ground coriander
½ tsp chilli powder
150ml water
375g ready-made puff pastry
Milk, for glazing and sealing

OK, if you have time to make the puff pastry, then knock yourself out and go for it. Otherwise here's the speedier route.

Step 1: In a large pot over a medium to high heat, cook the lamb, chillies, onion, salt, garam masala, ground coriander and chilli powder with the water until it reaches a rolling simmer and the meat has changed colour to a light brown; break up the mince to check there are no flashes of raw lamb. You should allow at least 15 minutes for this step of the process. Once cooked, pour the liquid away and leave the meat to cool. Ideally, cook the day before filling the pastry so the flavours intensify.

Step 2: Roll the puff pastry out on a floured surface to a rectangle of 30cm x 40cm. Slice down the middle lengthways, ending up with two long pieces. Place the pieces on a large greased baking tray. Fill the middle of each the sheet lengthways with a generous portion of lamb, leaving enough pastry either side of the filling to fold over and envelop it. Seal the edge with a little milk, making sure none of the mixture escapes. Take a fork and lightly drag it in diagonal strokes across the top of the long pastry roll, then brush the surface with milk. Cut each strip into 7 or 8 individual parcels. Heat the oven to 180°/Gas 4.

Step 3: Bake the pastries for 15–20 minutes, turning the baking tin halfway through to allow the patties to cook evenly. Once the patties have a golden glaze and are puffed up, dish on to rack and allow them to rest for 10 minutes.

Serve with Vicki Chutney (page 42).

16. George's quality

*also delicious
a party of a

THE ELEGANT KEBAB

Often when one thinks about meat kebabs, great hunks of meaty indulgence spring to mind. Marinated chunks of meat strung together on skewers to be torn apart by the gnashing of teeth – this awakens the primal instinct of the hunter. However, there is an elegant alternative. With a smooth, charming and suave persona, the shami kebab combines street cool with understated confidence. Made from a mélange of masalas, gram flour, eggs and finely pounded lamb, these kebabs should be shaped into patties and then gently sautéed and partnered with an accompaniment of choice, such as Vicki Chutney (page 42).

The Elegant Kebab.
(if one actually exists!)

SHAMI KEBAB

Serves 4–6

500g lamb mince
Salt
4cm fresh root ginger, peeled
6 garlic cloves, peeled
1 tsp cumin seeds
4 green cardamom pods, seeds removed
1 tsp ground cinnamon

8 black peppercorns
1 onion, finely chopped
4 green chillies, chopped
120g gram (chickpea) flour
2 eggs, fork-whipped
Vegetable oil, enough for shallow-frying (around 5mm depth in a frying pan)

Boil the mince in a large pan with enough water just to cover the surface of the meat and with a large pinch of salt. Cook for around 20–25 minutes until the meat has cooked through, then drain it, place in a bowl and mash it into a fine paste. Set aside.

Pop the garlic, ginger, cumin seeds, cardamom seeds, cinnamon, peppercorns and chillies into a spice grinder or pestle and mortar and smash into a paste consistency. Tip into a bowl, add the meat, onion, chilli, flour and eggs, and work the ingredients over, squishing between your fingers and fists to create an evenly blended meaty dough. If the mix is too wet, add a little flour until it's pliable and not too sticky.

Smear oil on your hands and tear off golfball-sized chunks, shaping them into flattened rounds of about 2–3cm in depth. Heat oil in a large frying pan over a medium heat and fry the shami kebabs in batches, browning on both sides, cooking for about 5–6 minutes in total.

Serve with Vicky Chutney (page 42) or Guddu's favourite (page 87).

GUDDU'S FAVOURITE CHUTNEY

This is a great dipping and spooning chutney – one of the many to choose from at our family shindigs. It's quick, simple and incredibly versatile, and it will often be used as a side dish, glistening next to a gentle hill of basmati rice. However, its most popular residence tends to be next to the street food enjoyed by Guddu Chachu.

SWEET AND SOUR TOMATO CHUTNEY

Makes enough for the Shami Kebabs

2 large tomatoes, chopped
2 garlic cloves, peeled
2cm fresh root ginger, peeled and roughly chopped
2 green chillies
Salt to taste
2 tbsp lime juice
3 tsp sugar
½ tsp tamarind concentrate
½ tsp toasted fennel seeds

Take all the ingredients and do one thing with them. Blend them in a food processor. Done. You can pretty it up with a couple of fennel fronds or coriander leaves.

JUMPER SOUP

Known as the Switzerland of the East, the foothills of the Himalayas are heart-stoppingly beautiful. Jagged peaks are surrounded by lush verdant forests and emerald lakes are fed by glaciers; single-gauge railways snake their way around vertiginous cliffs dotted by hill stations occupied by the British Raj during the stinking-hot months of summer. The stations are perched in their lofty, cool mountain retreats away from the *gupshup* (chit-chat or gossip) of the city, strung out like a jade necklace across the Himalayan range and offering a haven of clean air and tranquillity. Settled as the summer headquarters for the Punjab government until 1876, the Murree hill station in a corner of the north-west Himalayas was known as the Queen of Hills, and offered my uncle Stan and various siblings a rare holiday break. Wearing a jumper was a novelty, as were the landscape, the people and the food, all in stark contrast to the streets of Stan's Sindhi Province.

Here, traditionally cooling ingredients, such as yoghurt, were used to warm you up. Hot karhi was a welcome addition to the menu, a smooth yoghurt-based soup spiced with popping mustard seeds and the curiously named asafoetida. It's deliciously simple, a great alternative to cream of mushroom, and it warms the body and enchants the soul.

"deliciously simple"

KARHI

Serves 4–6

3 tbsp gram (chickpea) flour

500ml cool water

400ml natural yoghurt, fork whipped and at room temperature
(I like to use one with 10% fat)

½ tsp turmeric powder

1 tsp sugar

1 tsp salt

1 tsp black mustard seeds

2 tbsp extra virgin olive oil

2cm fresh root ginger, peeled and chopped into matchsticks

2 green chillies, finely chopped

8 curry leaves

¼ tsp asafoetida

Coriander leaves, chopped, to dress

Sift the flour into a bowl and combine with 60ml of the water to create a smooth paste. Tip in the rest of the water and keep whisking to avoid any lumps forming. Add the yoghurt, turmeric, sugar and salt and keep whisking; it's essential that the mix is velvety and even. Decant into a saucepan and, over a medium heat, stir constantly and bring to the boil. Reduce the heat and simmer for approximately 10 minutes, stirring regularly.

In a separate frying pan, sauté the mustard seeds in the oil until they pop, then immediately add the ginger, chillies and curry leaves. Fry for 3–4 minutes until everything has darkened a few shades. Drop in the asafoetida, mix thoroughly and combine with the simmering karhi. Muddle the ingredients, remove from the heat and dress with the chopped coriander leaves.

KARACHI'S CAFÉ CULTURE (I)

The evening streets of Karachi bustled like a disturbed ants' nest. Hawkers busked their street goodies, puncturing the warm air with scents of fresh flaky bohri samosas, fried river fish, lamb kebabs and the unmistakable aroma of the dancing partners ginger and garlic as they sizzled together in harmony in great bare skillets hovering over gas-fired stoves. Street lamps twinkled over the busy Pakistanis as they strolled, hurried, told jokes, swapped gossip, embraced friends and ate animatedly. Cool lassi-filled glasses washed down chilli-infused pakoras and ginger chicken. A young Guddu Chachu would glide through these social streets with smoothed hair, cologne stinging his freshly shaved face. Wearing his smartest shirt, he greeted friends with a customary kiss and ended the day with a treat: a leg of chicken stung with ginger and sesame, and a glass of Murree beer. He glanced up at the stars, sucking in the romantic mix of food, salty air and good company, his youthful confidence convincing him that this world was his for the taking. He sank his teeth into the tender chicken and tasted desire and hope.

GUDDU'S CHICKEN

Serves 4 as an appetiser

1kg chicken on the bone: legs, thighs, drumsticks
A little olive oil
1 tbsp toasted sesame seeds, to dress
Half a lemon, to serve

For the marinade paste
3 tbsp ginger paste (see page 93)
2 tbsp garlic paste (see page 93)
2 tbsp lemon juice
1 tbsp ground coriander
2 tsp chilli powder
Salt and pepper

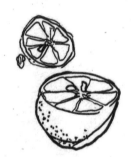

Mix all the marinade ingredients in a large bowl, seasoning well. Score the chicken pieces with a sharp knife to a depth of 5mm and massage the marinade into the chicken. Cover and refrigerate for a couple of hours (overnight is better).

Either over charcoals or under a grill set to medium, place the chicken pieces on a rack with a drip tray underneath and grill for 10 minutes on both sides. Remove from the heat and keep them on the rack, allowing them to rest for a couple of minutes until the juices have drained a little. Now use the 'drip juices' to baste the chicken, brush with a little olive oil and cook for a further 3–4 minutes. When done, scatter the toasted sesame seeds all over the chicken, covering well.

Best served hot with a squeeze of lemon juice.

GINGER PASTE

15cm fresh root ginger, peeled and roughly chopped
4 tbsp water

Bung the water and ginger in a blender and pulse until smooth. Transfer straight into an airtight container and refrigerate. Keeps for 3–4 days.

GARLIC PASTE

5 garlic bulbs, cloves separated and peeled
4 tbsp water

Pop the garlic and water into a blender and pulse until smooth. Pour into an airtight container and refrigerate. Keeps for 3–4 days.

KARACHI'S CAFÉ CULTURE (II)

Karachi's café culture and street scene was perhaps where young Stanley Peters felt most comfortable. It was an environment where social structures and class divides were reduced to a relaxed informal space where people could just 'be'. Café George was where they could watch the world and enjoy delicious inventions created by its Parsi (from 'Persian') owners. Through these kitchen doors emerged eloquently spiced dishes designed to surprise and delight. With no rush to be anywhere special, after Stan's working day at the Holy Family Hospital, he and his friends would meet at George's café. Wearing slick partings and youthful arrogance, they would hope to be spotted by a passing film scout and asked to feature in the next blockbuster to be made at Eastern Studios. But at George's the starring roles were already taken, and amongst the repertoire was a classic favourite – a whole chicken tenderly marinated in a blend of freshly ground spices. Left to rest and relax for a couple of hours, it was then slow-baked until its juices ran clear and diners could no longer fend off the hunger inspired by its splendid aroma. Café George sadly no longer exists, but the spirit of this bygone institution lives on in its recipes. Stanley enjoyed this chicken with a simple Desi Salad (see page 181). There's no other way to eat it.

GEORGE'S SLOW-COOKED CHICKEN

Serves up to 4

1 large chicken (2kg), skinned
4 garlic cloves, peeled
6cm fresh root ginger, peeled
  and grated
4 green chillies, chopped
1 tsp ground cumin
½ tsp ground cloves
½ tsp ground cinnamon

1 tsp ground coriander
1 tsp coriander seeds,
  smashed
60ml lemon juice
50ml olive oil
½ tsp cayenne pepper
Zest of 1 lemon
Salt and pepper

Score the chicken across the legs, thighs and breast approximately 2cm deep. Line a deep baking tray with enough foil to cover the bird.

Put the garlic, grated ginger, chillies, cumin, cloves, cinnamon, ground coriander and coriander seeds, lemon juice and oil into a blender and pulse until you have a paste.

Rub the paste all over the chicken, making sure the mix penetrates the slashes and the cavity has also been covered. Once smothered with the spice paste, lay the chicken in the middle of the foil-lined tray. Fold up the sides of the foil and crimp at the top, concealing the bird. Leave to marinate in a fridge for at least 2 hours, or overnight.

Heat the oven to 200°C/Gas 6. Open the chicken's foil suit, sprinkle the cayenne pepper and lemon zest over the bird, then reseal. Put in the oven and bake for an hour, then open up the package and spoon the chicken juices over the bird. Leave uncovered to cook for another 20–30 minutes, basting regularly. Pierce the thickest part of the leg and check the juices are running clear. It's ready … attack it!

INDIAN OCEAN KING FISH

Served in restaurants dotted around the Indian Ocean, the popular king fish is often found swimming in a sea of tomatoes and coriander surrounded by spice minnows such as cardamom and chilli. It's a dish with a grown-up taste. Far from the chaos of the bazaar, it is more likely to be found navigating its way through shoals of restaurants staffed by waiters in white mess jackets. A young man like my uncle Stan may have felt this was a 'coming of age' dish. It was the taste of an honest wage and the first fruit of economic

independence in his hometown, Karachi. He knew, like his brothers had discovered, that his future resided overseas, and these simple pleasures were a foretaste of what he hoped was to come.

I love the texture and taste of this fish. A buttery meaty form, it's the perfect straight man to this curry's cheeky persona. However, I've found it to be elusive on Blighty's fish counters. For the dedicated, it can be picked up in Asian supermarkets. However, for the convenient cook, I'd recommend salmon or tuna steaks.

KING FISH CURRY

Serves 4–6

1kg king fish steaks or similar firm fish steaks

For the curry paste
5 large tomatoes
5 green chillies
250g fresh coriander leaves

For the curry sauce
5 tbsp olive oil
8 green cardamom pods
4 bay leaves
1 tbsp garlic paste (see page 93)
1 tbsp ginger paste (see page 93)

½ tsp cayenne pepper
2 tbsp ground coriander
½ tsp turmeric powder
½ tsp dried fenugreek leaves, finger-crumbled
175ml water
Salt

Creating the paste is easy: simply blend all the ingredients together. In a pan large enough to poach the fish in a single layer, heat the oil over a medium temperature and sauté the cardamom pods and bay leaves for a minute until they've darkened in colour. Add the curry paste to the pan and cook for a couple of minutes, then drop in the rest of the ingredients, stirring and seasoning well.

Carefully layer in the fish and poach for 10–15 minutes on a low heat until the fish is firm enough to flake (test with a fork). Gently stir and add a little more water if necessary to avoid the mix sticking, then simmer for a further 5 minutes. King Curry packs a wicked aromatic punch and it'll fill your senses with the Karachi coastline.

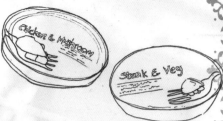

'WHATEVER YOU WANT, THE ANSWER'S NO'

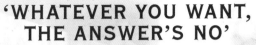

It wasn't the warmest greeting the shiny-haired, twenty-something Stan had ever received. After all, this was supposed to be genteel England with its mild manners and polite pretensions. He stood in front of the white-coated sales assistant clutching his Fray Bentos tinned meat pie and thought better of asking her the price. He knew if he'd spoken, a splurge of confusion and anger would have come out of his mouth. He caught her eye and she darted hers over his shoulder to the queue behind him and shooed him away with an absent hand. It wouldn't be the last time he'd stare prejudice in the face, and one day he'd square up to it and teach it a lesson. Since that episode he has steered clear of tinned meals and opted for a diet of fresh ingredients. He longed for the texture of tender, juicy red meat in delicious brown gravy, and whilst working the factory line at Champion Spark Plugs, he traded recipes for smokes and discovered what is undoubtedly the central jewel in his culinary crown.

I call it Passanda – the original. It features flattened pieces of lamb that give it a crumbly, fragile texture, inhabiting a sepia lake of fragrant jus. It's not to be confused with its wide-boy cousin often served in Indian restaurants, which parades chicken intoxicated by a jaundiced cream fruit splodge, which would perhaps be more at home in a bell-shaped glass fringed with tiny umbrellas. Passanda's velvety richness lends the senses a tone of Mughal opulence, and the spice hit throws a flurry of elegant jabs.

PASSANDA – THE ORIGINAL

Serves up to 6

1kg lamb or mutton fillet

2 onions, sliced

3 tbsp olive oil

5cm fresh root ginger, peeled and roughly chopped

3 green chillies, chopped

6 green cardamom pods

2 black cardamom pods

4 cloves

2 tbsp garlic paste (page 93)

2 tsp curry powder

½ tsp cayenne pepper

2 tbsp ground coriander

200ml water

1 tsp garam masala (see page 46)

500ml natural yoghurt, fork whipped and at room temperature
 (I like to use one with 10% fat)

Cut the lamb into pieces about 7.5cm long and 1cm thick. Place the pieces on a chopping board, cover the meat with cling film and beat with a meat mallet or rolling pin into thin slices – think 'minute steak' depth. Mutton works better, but if using lean lamb fillet, reduce the overall cooking time by 20–30 minutes. This is the passanda part of the dish.

In a large frying pan or wok, fry the onions in the oil until soft and translucent. Add the ginger, chillies, cardamom and cloves, and cook for 2–3 minutes until the ginger has relaxed. Pour in the garlic paste and sprinkle over the curry, cayenne and coriander, and stir for 3–4 minutes until the onions have soaked up all the spices. Slip in the passanda and mix thoroughly, making sure the meat is covered with the mix.

Brown the lamb, then cover the pan and let it simmer on a low heat for 10 minutes. Add 200ml water and cook for an hour, checking to make sure the lamb isn't sticking to the pan, adding more water to loosen if necessary. Sprinkle in the garam masala and cook for another 20 minutes. Spoon in the yoghurt and carefully stir, making sure it doesn't split. Simmer for another 20–30 minutes, stirring frequently. If the lamb is tender and the oil is rising to the surface of the curry, it's ready.

Eat with flatbread – it's the only way to scoop up the thick gravy. It's great with a helping of Kachumbar (page 35) and Raitha (page 224).

INSEPARABLE PARTNERS

Fred and Ginger, Reagan and Thatcher, Morecambe and Wise, the Krankies – all created formidable partnerships, duos to be reckoned with. Each was incomplete without the other, and this is the philosophy adopted by Stanley Peters when he says, 'Curry needs rice.' It's a partnership of ingredients that shouldn't be separated, but rather actively encouraged, particularly with Stan's basmati rice that comes embroidered with shiny green peas that pop and peak like little starlets. The role of rice? Well, apart from its obvious use in mopping up gravy, it absorbs the flavour of the curry it's hitched with, adding texture and depth whilst introducing complementary flavours. The sparkling petit pois provide a touch of innocent sweetness and a little crunch. I've tried various methods to produce rice that's perfect, fluffy and proud, without any of the gluey starchiness resembling wallpaper paste. Stan's approach, however, has done me very well, so out of family duty I recommend his method to you.

MATTAR CHAWAL

Serves 4

4 tbsp olive oil
Half an onion, finely sliced
1 tsp coriander seeds
6 green cardamom pods
1 tsp cumin seeds
2 bay leaves
250g basmati rice, rinsed
1 tsp salt
Handful of frozen peas
Pepper

In a large frying pan or wok, warm the oil over a medium heat and fry the onion until translucent: it'll take just a couple of minutes. Drop in the whole spices and bay leaves and stir for a minute or two until the pan becomes aromatic. Now add the rice and coat the grains, glazing them with the oil. Add salt to the pan, then pour in water to approximately 1cm above the surface of rice. The mix will cackle as the water mocks the oil. Stir. You'll need to keep adding water to the pan (just above the rice plateau) until the rice has absorbed the liquid. About 15 minutes into cooking, throw in the frozen peas and mix, allowing them to shine and pop through the rice. After 5 minutes, check the rice and peas, season with pepper. The grains should be soft, not al dente, and the peas should be pert and plucky. The whole affair should take approximately 20 minutes.

STAN'S SWEET TOOTH

Perhaps he was indulged as the youngest, maybe he was just born with it, or perhaps he's developed a highly tuned set of taste buds. Either way, my uncle Stan loves his sweet stuff. But it's not just any sweet-smelling or sweet-looking distraction that appeals to him, it's desserts that have been lovingly prepared and cooked. I think I've inherited his sweet affliction, enjoying Indian-style pieces of mithai (fudge,) and milk-sweetened desserts popping with nuts and raisins, some gooey, some loose, but all moreish and irresistibly yummy.

Seviyan is a family favourite, and has no bigger advocate than Guddu Chachu. Once the main courses are cleared and the desserts are being laid up, he switches to sport mode, and with the tenacity of a Formula One driver he manages pole position every time.

This dish isn't an obvious dessert given that it uses rice noodles, but it hits notes of smoky toffee-ness, basking in rich velvety milk. The texture of crushed nuts and chewy raisins and cranberries could lull you into a momentary sense of 'being good', but banish those thoughts and get real. Let your inner kid loose and get stuck into this dish with gusto.

SEVIYAN

Serves 4–6 in smallish portions

1 tbsp unsalted butter

50g vermicelli rice noodles

500ml whole milk

225g condensed milk

3 tsp sugar

3 green cardamom pods, seeds removed and pummelled
    into powder

2 tbsp mixed raisins and cranberries

2 tbsp mixed pecan and pistachio nuts, crushed
    (not powdered)

Using a medium-sized pan, melt the butter over a low heat
and, before it starts frothing, fry the vermicelli until golden
brown. Take the pan off the heat. In a separate pan, boil
the milk, then add the condensed milk, vermicelli, sugar and
cardamom powder, and cook for 3–4 minutes until the vermicelli (seviyan) becomes soft. Whilst hot, spoon into bowls
and sprinkle the nuts and fruit over the surface.

Stan's seviyan can also be eaten cold.

CRICKET WHITES

Pulling on his whites and pads, my uncle Stan didn't just experience the momentary happiness that most of the Sunday League Cricket amateurs felt: a few hours away from the missus and a couple of pints in the pub afterwards with the lads. For him the moment wasn't fleeting, it was significantly deeper. He lingered over the feeling of acceptance, that now finally he could play for a team (aptly named Technicolour) regardless of his skin colour, and that the team didn't drink in a pub proudly displaying its prejudice in the signage below the landlord's name: 'No Blacks, Irish or Gypsies'. Technicolour accepted him for who he was: a fast bowler and an opening batsman. He savoured the confidence in his ability to wreak havoc with fielders, reversing and switching his batting strokes, sending the visiting team stretching and leaping as they desperately tried to pluck the cherry-leather ball out of the air. Levelling out the speed bumps in the ground before him with his bat, he returned to the crease with pride, knowing he'd send the next over into orbit.

My enduring memory of this seasonal tradition was the break where the teams would retire to the pavilion for 'tea', which really meant curly sandwiches concealing rubber cheese and watery pickle, crisps that were soft and chicken drumsticks that were tougher than an East End prize fighter. Stretching out on the edge of the clipped

cricket lawn, my cousins, brother and I waited for the crack of the lid, as Tupperware jam-packed with chicken and surrounded by aromatic rice with fat black cardamom pods the size of grapes was opened. Tender chicken fell into the arms of whole spices such as cloves and cumin seeds, each grain of rice separate and unstuck, bearing the yellow tinge of curried chicken and bright green bullets of happily shining petit pois. Spoonfuls were balanced on to flimsy plastic plates and Coke fizzed into transparent cups. Silence fell among our camp as we tucked into the Cricket Chicken with plastic forks and hungry fingers. As I watched my uncle Stan's bushy Ian Botham moustache waggle as he chewed on a chicken thigh, I detected another emotion: total pleasure.

Enjoyed cold or hot, this recipe is more than just a set of ingredients – each morsel is flavoured with pride … *HOWZAT!*

CRICKET CHICKEN

Serves 6

4 tbsp vegetable oil

2 medium onions, sliced

6 black cardamom pods

6 cloves

1 cinnamon quill

1 tbsp medium curry powder

2 tsp ground coriander

3 bay leaves

1 tsp turmeric powder

1kg chicken thighs and drumsticks, skinless

2 litres water

6 green cardamom pods

1 tsp cumin seeds

1 tbsp garlic paste (see page 93)

1 tbsp ginger paste (see page 93)

3 green chillies, chopped

Salt

500g basmati rice, rinsed

This recipe has 3 glorious stages:

Make the chicken stock.

Cook the rice with the stock (make the pulao).

Combine the rice and chicken.

Make the stock (yakhni). In a large stockpot over a medium heat, warm 2 tsbp of the oil and fry one of the onions until soft. Stir in the black cardamom, cloves, cinnamon, curry powder, coriander, bay leaves and turmeric and cook for a couple of minutes until the mix has become dry and fragrant. Now add the chicken pieces and rouse all the ingredients, cooking for 5 minutes or until the chicken has browned and released its juices. Pour in the water, turn the heat to low and cook for 1½–2 hours or until the chicken is very tender, almost falling off the bone. Drain the yakhni into a separate bowl, removing any bits, and reserve the chicken for later.

Make the pulao. Using another large stockpot, fry the remaining onion in the remaining oil over a medium heat until browned. Mix in the green cardamom and cumin seeds. Now add the garlic and ginger pastes, cooking until the mixture is bubbling, then drop in the chilli. Agitate the pot and your nostrils should get a chilli hit. Season with salt and tip in the rice, coating everything with whole spices and the sheen of oil. Ladle in the stock, covering the rice an inch above the surface. Reduce the heat and cook for 20 minutes or until the rice is almost done. Keep ladling in stock to prevent the rice from sticking and burning.

Combine the chicken and rice. The rice should be 80 per cent cooked. Add the chicken pieces and cook for a further 10 minutes until the rice is cooked through and has absorbed all the stock. The chicken should be just intact and tender, daring to peel away from the bone.

Serve with Raitha (page 224). If eating it hot, complement it with a runny curry such as Comfort Daal (page 76).

LOVE STORY

Uncle Stanley glimpsed his future every day. It felt so close yet elusively unobtainable.

He'd been wounded deeply by a dart from cupid's bow and the object of his desire was an angelic vision of Cockney charm with high cheekbones, an East End brogue and razor-sharp wit. He worked the line at Black & Decker and she was office staff. His charm offensive consisted of Hai Karate aftershave, slicked hair, flared collars and a movie-star moustache. Stan wasn't alone in his admiration for Doreen Crew's looks and character, but he fought valiantly in the battleground of love until he captured her heart. They were soulmates for over

thirty years, competing against ugly looks from strangers, whose eyes questioned their mixed-race union. Many doubted that this cross-cultural marriage could work, but in the end their devotion to each other silenced the cynics. I remember my aunt as a woman with joie de vivre. She had a taste for curry and a weakness for quality rum, both of which she enjoyed until her early departure from us all. She acquired a voracious appetite for Stan's curry, and amongst her favourites was an old classic: korma. Unlike the insipid impostor on many an Indian take-away menu, this dish didn't contain cream or nuts and come with a 'mild' rating. Instead its intense deep flavours and rich sauce set off a round of delightful fireworks, as if our taste buds were celebrating some auspicious occasion. I call it 'kismet korma' (which means it's 'meant to be'), because for my auntie Doreen it truly was love at first bite.

KISMET KORMA

Serves 4–6

2 onions, sliced
4 tbsp olive oil
1kg boneless mutton, diced
6 green cardamom pods
2 tsp fennel seeds, pounded into powder
1 tsp ground cumin
1 tbsp ground coriander
1 tsp chilli powder
8 cloves
8 peppercorns
1½ tsp salt
400g natural yoghurt, fork whipped and at room temperature
    (I like to use one with 10% fat)
5 green chillies
250g tinned chopped tomatoes
500ml water
1 tsp kewra (aka screwpine or pandanus water) or rosewater
Coriander leaves, chopped

Cook this the night before you want to eat it.

Fry up the onions in the oil until crispy and golden, then set them aside on kitchen paper to dry out. Keep the oil. In the same pan, using the onion oil, brown off the mutton, adding the cardamom, fennel, cumin, coriander and chilli powder. When the mutton is browned, drop in the cloves, peppercorns and salt and cook over a low heat for around 30 minutes, until the meat has started to cook in its own juices and the mix is looking darker. Blend the yoghurt, chillies, reserved fried onions and tomatoes, turning it into a paste. Add the paste into the pan and swish the ingredients around until everything is coated. Turn up the heat to medium and cook for a further 1½ hours, making sure you stir frequently. To stop the ingredients drying out and sticking to the bottom of the pan, add the water at intervals. The curry shouldn't be too runny. Just before serving, add a teaspoon of kewra or rosewater.

It takes time but classics like these shouldn't be rushed. Serve with rotis or rice and garnish with chopped coriander. Superb with Channa Masala (see page 194).

PUNK GOURD

He held two punked-up cucumbers. With their studs and blunt spikes, they looked like some feral vegetable conceived in the imagination of an unhinged scientist. He smiled as he sensed the distrust in my eyes. How could such an ugly-looking vegetable produce a dish of such glorious proportions? When compared to the beauty of a shiny aubergine, the floral arrangement of a cauliflower or the innocence of a potato, this bitter gourd looked like the black sheep of the family, the wayward cousin no one talks about. It would take serious rehabilitation and the patience of someone special to turn this gnarly object into a gourmand experience.

Guddu Chachu introduced me to the vegetable known across his homeland as karela and showed me the simple ingenuity required to turn this ugly duckling into a gracious swan. Unlike in British cuisine, bitter gourds are commonly used across Asia and they're susceptible to various interpretations. Here's Guddu Chachu's version, sweet and sour with a delicious piquancy. He's laboured over it and in return I've loved it.

KARELA CURRY

Serves 4 as a side dish or 2–3 as a main

500g bitter gourd
   (approximately 6)
Salt
3 tbsp olive oil
1 onion, sliced
½ tsp turmeric powder
1 tsp ground coriander

3 medium tomatoes, chopped
2 green chillies, finely sliced
⅓ tsp chilli powder
100ml water
½ tsp tamarind concentrate
Coriander leaves, to dress

Peel the skin from the bitter gourd, slice through the middle and scoop out the seeds from the centre. Chop the flesh into chunks, put in a bowl and sprinkle with salt. Cover and leave for 3 hours, or overnight if possible. Wash thoroughly – this is really important as they'll stay very bitter if not rinsed well – and pat dry.

In a large frying pan or wok, heat the oil over a medium temperature and brown the onion. Add the turmeric, ground coriander and tomatoes, cooking for a couple of minutes, then drop in the chillies and chilli powder, pour in the water and drip in the tamarind concentrate. Turn the heat down and stir the ingredients together, frying the masala for 5–8 minutes until everything has combined, the turmeric has lost some of its initial pungency and the mix is a little drier. Add the bitter gourd and cook for 15 minutes, stirring gently. The chunks will recede and shrink a bit, which is normal. Test the bitter gourd by piercing with a fork. If the fork meets no resistance, the dish is ready to be served. Sprinkle with fresh coriander leaves.

An alternative approach is to mix this dish with keema (see page 119 but leave out the aloo). If you want to try this, reduce the karela cooking time by 10 minutes as you'll need to cook it with the keema for about 10 minutes.

SHIFT WORK

'Sorry, love, it's just chicken curry today,' my Auntie Doreen said. 'Stan and I have been on shifts this week, so it's all we've had time to make.' She rolled her eyes heavenward. 'And you know your Guddu Chachu can't be without his curry, bloody Asian,' she mocked with a twinkle in her eye. They'd been together for over twenty years; she knew his every foible and he knew hers. She worked in hospitality at a local hotel and he landed a job at Heathrow Airport, exchanging shifts and snatching moments together. They developed certain dishes to fit into their working pattern, which often meant tag cooking: one would start preparing a meal whilst the other took over to finish it, ready for consumption between shifts. I remember this particular chicken dish as it uses a *shorba* method (cooking with water), reducing spices and ingredients into a clingy, yet relatively runny texture, resulting in juicy, tender chicken thighs, the meat requiring little persuasion to melt off the bone into a spice-rich lagoon. It can be made using a glorious combination of teamwork, allowing both parties to add a little flourish to the recipe, or one can fly solo and own it completely.

In my case, Guddu Chachu started it, Auntie Doreen finished it and I showed it no mercy, barely allowing it to touch the sides. It's a beautifully simple recipe for those juggling time and tasks. It can be layered with spices and combines a depth of flavour only achieved by cooking meat on the bone. In short, the ingredients do all the work, so you can spend life's most precious commodity at will.

116

SHIFT CHICKEN CURRY

Serves 4, with plain white boiled rice

8 chicken thighs, skinless, each one slashed to a depth of 2cm
2 small onions, sliced
2 green chillies, finely chopped
3 garlic cloves, smashed and chopped
2 tbsp ginger paste (see page 93)
½ tsp turmeric powder
½ tsp fennel seeds
1 tsp ground coriander
1 cinnamon quill, snapped in half
2 x 400g tins chopped tomatoes with juice
1 litre water
20 fresh curry leaves
½ tsp garam masala (see page 46)
Squeeze of lemon

Using a large stock pot, combine everything apart from the garam masala and lemon juice (add this at the end). The chicken thighs should be smothered in the watery ingredients. Make sure the coriander and turmeric are fully mixed in with the tomatoes and water, working the thin paste into the slashed chicken. The cuts in the chicken will help the spices seep into the meat. Over a medium heat, cook uncovered for 1–1½ hours, or until the chicken is tender, stirring every now and then. The curry gravy will have reduced into a deep, velvety, crimson sauce, intensifying the flavours, and the chicken will be holding on to the bone for dear life.

Take off the heat, sprinkle in the garam masala and squeeze in a touch of lemon juice. Enjoy this low-maintenance dish with plain boiled rice.

A COMFORTING CLASSIC

Some dishes follow you throughout your life. They're as constant as family photo albums – they're always there and every now and then you find yourself revisiting them, reminiscing and savouring the moments. There's comfort and delight in the experience.

I was talking with my uncle Stan, and he shared some valuable travel tips with me. He covered his journey across India, Thailand, Cambodia and Vietnam, and wistfully reflected on his travels with his late wife. Now in his retirement years, he pursued an intentionally busy life, travelling, playing cricket as a veteran and teaching the kids 'a thing or two about speed bowling'. His hair as white as clouds, eyes reflecting adventure with hints of youthful energy, he paused mid-sentence as he described villages on the Mekong Delta. 'Put-ther [son], you've not eaten. You've got to eat.'

Walk into any Asian household and you've entered into a covenant to eat whatever's on offer. On this occasion it was a shared love for an old classic, keema aloo. It's a dish that has tracked both mine and Stan's lives from boy to man; wonderfully simple, relatively quick and deliciously satisfying, it's enjoyed by meat-eating households across the Indian subcontinent.

The blend of layered spices transforms lamb or beef mince (dependent on your preference) into pellets of succulent meat, saturated in the warming tones of garam masala and juicy onions, partnered with garlic shavings and the powdered elegance of coriander. The combination softens the floury white potatoes, ready to be mushed under the pressure of flatbread between thumb and forefinger. Sweet green peas peer from the mince temptingly. It would be easy to label this dish as meat and potatoes, but for me and my uncle Stan it's a staple family favourite, and not just for the boys either.

KEEMA ALOO

Serves 4

2 tbsp oil

2 medium onions, chopped

6 black peppercorns

1 black cardamom pod

½ tsp cumin seeds

1 tsp ginger paste (see page 93)

1 tsp garlic paste (see page 93)

2 tomatoes, chopped

500g lean lamb or beef mince

Salt

½ tsp chilli powder

1 tsp ground coriander

1 tbsp curry powder

1 tsp garam masala (see page 46)

250g potatoes, peeled and chopped into chunks

2 green chillies, chopped

Handful of fresh coriander leaves, chopped

In a large pot over a medium heat, warm the oil, then sauté the onions until opaque. Add the peppercorns, cardamom, cumin seeds, ginger and garlic pastes and tomatoes. Stir well and cook for 2–3 minutes until the mix has dried a little. Pop in the mince and brown, then mix everything up and cook for around 10 minutes until the meat has released its juices and the pot smells fragrant and is making you hungry. Season with salt, pitch in the powdered spices – chilli, coriander, curry and garam masala – tip in the potatoes and chopped chillies and add enough water to cover the surface of the ingredients. Cover and cook for around 30 minutes or until the potatoes have softened and cooked through. Uncover and cook over a high heat for 5 minutes, reducing the gravy until it's sticking to the meat and tatties.

Sprinkle the coriander leaves on the keema aloo and serve with naans.

THE ORIGINAL SMOOTHIE

We sat opposite each other and Uncle Stan's face wrinkled into a smile as I licked my fingers clean from the meaty juices of the smooth lamb shami kebabs and red coriander chutney. I glugged down the velvety thickness of the lemon-sweetened yoghurt (invented long before the smoothie), wiping my lips with the back of my hand. He let a chuckle escape, followed by a mini burp caused by the samosa he'd been dipping into the same chutney.

'I loved lassi when I was a kid, I still do.' He watched the cold tears of the glass collect on the white Formica table of the *chaat* (snack) house in Slough, conveniently located just around the corner from his flat. Allowing his taste buds to reminisce for a short while, he signalled his order of chapattis, a portion of mattar paneer and saag ghosht to the passing waiter. He indulged himself with a mango version of my lassi, his eyes flickering with youth as he drained the glass in a series of large glugs. From boy to man, lassi is the only drink I'd risk fisticuffs for. It quenches, satisfies and excites, coming in different varieties ranging from fruity, salty to sweet, and satiates over a billion people across the globe. So join the party ... it's never too late.

LASSI

Serves a thirsty duo

For sweet lassi
300ml natural yoghurt
150ml milk
4 tsp sugar, to taste
Squeeze of fresh lemon
Sprinkling of fresh ground cardamom
For plain lassi, replace sugar with a touch of salt

For mango lassi
250ml natural yoghurt
100ml milk
4 tsp sugar, to taste
200ml mango flesh, peeled and chopped

Apart from the cardamom for the plain lassi, pop everything into a blender and pulse until the mix is rich and velvety. Pour into refrigerated glasses. Dust the plain lassi with cardamom.

RUNNY CURRY

As I watch my uncle Stan eat with the rest of his silver-haired brothers, I catch glimpses of what their boyhood must have been like. They are camped around the dinner table relishing every mouthful, encouraging each other to eat just one more chapatti, and I spot flashes of youthful energy in their exuberance as they tear meat from the chops, leaving stacks of bleached white bones in their wake. They mop up rich runny onion and clove gravy with fluffy white rice and scoop up dry vegetable curry with freshly pressed flatbread. For them, meat on the bone is the richest and tastiest source of protein, cooked slowly over a low heat for a couple of hours. The lamb melts off, actually requiring little effort. The ritual of sucking every last morsel from the bone is a childhood pleasure, avoiding waste and somehow satisfying a deeper primal urge.

These typical family meals consist of three dishes: a runny curry, a dry vegetable recipe and rice, serenaded by rotis or naans. Runny lamb chop curry scores every time. It's a simple one-pot wonder which, once on the stove, requires little attention. An occasional stir and a sniff test prepare your belly for what's in store. You don't need to strip the bones clean, but my guess is you'll want to.

122

LAMB CHOP CURRY

Serves 4, eaten with fluffy rice

3 tbsp corn oil
1 onion, finely chopped
5cm fresh root ginger, peeled and roughly chopped
4 garlic cloves, crushed
3 fresh green chillies, chopped
12 mutton chops, trimmed of fat
1 tbsp coriander seeds, crushed
1 tsp cumin seeds, toasted and crushed
400g tin chopped tomatoes
1 tbsp curry powder
1 tbsp ground coriander
150g natural yoghurt, fork whipped and at room temperature
 (I like to use yoghurt with 10% fat)
1 tsp garam masala (see page 46)
Salt
Sprinkling of coriander leaves

In a large pot, heat the oil over a medium temperature and fry the onion until slightly golden. Add the garlic, ginger and chillies, cooking for a minute. Turn the heat down and add the chops, browning on both sides for 10 minutes until the meat releases some of its juices and bubbles. Add the coriander and cumin seeds, cover and leave to cook for a further 5 minutes. In a blender create a masala paste by pouring in the tinned tomatoes, curry and coriander and blitzing.

Tip the masala paste into the cooking pot and stir thoroughly, season with salt. Cover and cook for a further 45 minutes, stirring regularly, making sure the consistency doesn't stick or get too thick, adding a little water if required to loosen it. Spoon in the yoghurt, combining the ingredients between each spoonful, making sure the yoghurt doesn't split. Add the garam masala, stir everything, cover and cook for another 20–30 minutes until the lamb is super tender and swathed in gorgeous runny brown gravy with the surface glistening like sun on the sea. Sprinkle with coriander leaves.

Overwhelm this curry with rice and peas, a fresh tomato salad and hot Chapattis (page 172).

MEATY BROTH
– A BEAR HUG OF A DISH

Stan's eyes wandered past my shoulder and into the distance as he recalled the dishes he missed from the home of his youth. His eyes were moist with nostalgia and a yearning for just another taste of the meaty broth known as haleem.

'It's definitely one of the dishes I miss most. It's so hard to find a good bowl of haleem these days,' he reminisced over the depth and warming texture of the dish often eaten in the winter months and in the northern, mountainous territories. It's a bowl of home comfort, a nutritious combination of lentils, shredded lamb and bulgur wheat. I first tasted haleem in the Himalayas in the hill station of Simla, the summer home of the British Raj, and it left a big impression on me. If food could cradle you, then this recipe has the ability to deliver an enormous bear hug. Its origins are reputed to be in the Caucasus, before it travelled across Persia and into northern India. Haleem has come a long way and it's only good manners to give it a try.

HALEEM

Serves up to 8

7 onions, sliced
   (keep in 3 piles: 4 onions, 2 onions and 1 onion)
250ml vegetable oil
2 tbsp ginger paste (see page 93)
2 tbsp garlic paste (see page 93)
8 garlic cloves, crushed and chopped
2 tsp turmeric powder
1 tbsp ground coriander
1 tbsp chilli powder
1kg boneless lamb, cut into 4cm cubes
250g bulgur wheat
250g mixed pulses, such as red and yellow lentils
Salt
2 litres water
1 tbsp garam masala (see page 46)
Mint leaves and lime wedges to serve

To start, fry the 4 sliced onions in a little of the oil until brown at the edges. Allow to cool, then mince in a blender.

   You'll need a large pot for the next stage. Heat the rest of the oil over a medium temperature and add the 2 sliced onions, frying until golden. Pour in the ginger and garlic pastes together with the crushed garlic and minced onions, drop in the turmeric, coriander and chilli powder, and stir-fry for a couple of minutes until the masala has darkened in colour. Add the lamb and brown all over for 10 minutes.

   Tip in the bulgur and mixed pulses, season with salt and flood with the water. Bring the water to the boil and then reduce the heat to low, cover and cook for 1½ hours. Stir regularly, making sure nothing sticks to the bottom.

Once the meat is tender, mash it with the back of a wooden spoon and cook for another 20 minutes. The oil should have risen to the top. Layer in the garam masala, allowing it to saturate for another 10 minutes. After 2 hours of cooking, the pot should be a heaving spiced lamb broth.

In a separate pan, fry the remaining sliced onion until crispy. Tip the onion over the surface of the haleem when it's served, then sprinkle with mint leaves and lime chunks. Eat with a spoon.

PART THREE
ABBU
(ALBERT PETERS)

ALBERT PETERS

'll fix you,' murmured Albert Peters, as the hot, stinging pain spread across his palm in the shape of the teacher's ruler.

Abbu's punishment was the result of the non-appearance of his homework. His response was to deliver the same degree of embarrassing pain, as his free hand gripped the spine of his thick study book and launched it, achieving mach speed as it homed in on the offending teacher's bald patch, leaving him to gulp for air as the book bounced off his reddening scalp. An eruption of gasps and laughter encouraged Abbu to make a quick exit and emerge into the Pakistani daylight as a classroom hero.

Hot-tempered, bold and fiery best describe his youthful temperament, and although the years have softened his character, these traits still accurately describe his love affair with food. He was the second eldest of seven and he would often be seen staring at the sky, watching the trail of jet-plane vapours, hoping that one day he would follow his dream of working with aircraft. At the smooth-faced age of fifteen, he progressed through his mechanical engineering apprenticeship to land a job at KLM Airlines. Working with his hands would be a way of life for him. He set them to lifting weights and body-building, his confidence and swagger blossoming in harmony with his expanding biceps, and he carried a no-nonsense approach to life. Fools avoided him, and his toughness was experienced by his younger siblings as he regulated their behaviour with the hairy side of his calloused hands. Yet despite his machismo, cupid struck twice, wounding him with a love of both food and a young, fair-skinned Pakistani beauty named Lorena.

Together they fed, loved and nurtured their children and, like many others, theirs became a story of migration. On 10 April 1968, the same day as the birth of his baby daughter, Reba, Albert made the solo flight to England, seeking to carve out an improved life for his family. He felt the cold Brummy air as he hammered away at his first job in a West Bromwich foundry. With twelve-hour shifts starting at 6am, the finish line was the pub, then a meal of home-cooked comforts with family relations. He sensed his British odyssey had further to go and he headed to West London to be closer to his younger brother, Victor. He settled in the shadow of the M4 in Brentford and worked the 'Gold Mile' of manufacturing on the Great Western Road.

A pattern of shiftwork spun him through various jobs starting at Brentford Nylons then onto United Biscuits and Firestone, grafting alongside fellow Asian and West Indian immigrants. Mates also worked the shop floor at Lucozade, Gillette and Martini. Now in the mid-1970s with his family over from Pakistan and having to feed extra mouths, he needed the overtime, which was abundant, as was optimism. Lunchtimes would be spent at Abbu's house, where the fortunate would be treated to Lorena's fried stuffed flatbread parathas. The grainy TV screen would sow woe or joy depending on how many wickets Pakistan or the West Indies had taken. As far back as I can remember, the house was always full. Food would arrive in waves and crash on palates with sparks of spice. Eyes would roll in food ecstasy, fingers would set to work raiding piles of tandoori chicken and fat kebabs, and teeth would tear at fresh roti bread. As a young boy, my abiding memory of Uncle Abbu's house is of colossal food generosity. Parties kicked into action with the assistance of bass bins thumping out a mix of bhangra beats and reggae, ending the evening with soporific ghazals (poetry sung in Urdu). This was the house of fun, and his food is so deliciously energetic it parties with your senses and commits you to gluttonous sin.

HEAVENLY FOOD

'Hail Mary, full of grace, the Lord is with thee …' Mass and chops.
Abbu was distinctly more enthusiastic about one than the other.
Sundays were truly heavenly for Abbu. It wasn't the aroma of incense
or the flowing robes worn by the Fathers or the cool, darkened church
that sparked his celestial interest, it was the careful preparation of
Sunday Chops. He truly believed these marinated pieces of lamb
had been blessed by the Trinity. As he mumbled his way through his
Hail Mary and the liturgies alongside his siblings, he couldn't take
his mind off the lust that ravaged his belly … surely there would be
penance to pay? His mind wandered to the wooden family lunch
table where he and his brothers and sisters would rip into Mama's
treats of perfectly cooked, tender lamb back chops. The masala
yoghurt mix would work its miraculous power deep into the meat
rinsed with lemon and peppered with vibrant coriander leaves. His
gastric soul performed Ave Marias whilst his taste buds erupted into
a chorus of hallelujahs. As he was nudged by his younger brother
to join the communion line he wondered, 'Is it possible for food to
be truly heavenly?' In my opinion the answer lies in Abbu's entrée
version of Mama's recipe, Divine Chops.

DIVINE CHOPS

Serves 4

12 lamb chops, fat trimmed

For the marinade

1 onion, roughly chopped
3 garlic cloves, peeled
6cm fresh root ginger, peeled and roughly chopped
2 green chillies
½ tsp garam masala (see page 46)
1 tsp turmeric powder
2 tsp ground coriander
1 tsp ground cumin

½ tsp ground cinnamon
150g natural yoghurt, fork whipped and at room temperature (I like to use yoghurt with 10% fat)
2 tsp salt
Juice of 1 lemon
Handful of fresh coriander leaves, chopped

Blend all the ingredients for the marinade in a food processor. You'll end up with a smooth paste. In a bowl, combine the chops and the marinade, cover and refrigerate for at least a couple of hours, or overnight if you've got the time.

Heat the oven to 180°C/Gas 4. Spread the marinade-smothered chops in a non-stick baking tin, cover with foil and cook for 30 minutes. After this time, the yoghurt and the meat's juices will have created a clearish 'water' – spoon this out as the chops need be dry. Cover and cook for a further 15 minutes, after which if there's more juice, spoon it off. Turn the chops over, leave them uncovered and cook for another 10 minutes. Once done, tear off a little with a fork. The meat should be tender and easy to pull off the bone.

Serve hot, rinsed with lemon and sprinkled with coriander. Accompany with a fresh, sharp Desi Salad (see page 181).

'YOU SCRUB THEM AND I'LL COOK THEM'

That was the deal his mother struck as Abbu begged her to cook prawn pilau. She wasn't fond of the prawn-cleansing process and she would only cook this family favourite if one of her brood volunteered to buy, scrub, peel and clean the bags of prawns required to satisfy the appetite of her Karachi clan. The delicate creamy texture of fresh prawns touched by bay leaves, coriander, lime and soft sweet peas in fine basmati rice would swell their appetite in preparation for the food scrum soon to follow.

Abbu's teenage bravado always ensured a negotiated price with the brutish-looking mongers at the fish market. Their bare, tattooed, sea-slimed arms grappled with their catch, sending decapitated heads into bins. Bloodied aprons smeared with aquaculture and sun-slaved tans completed their menacing look.

Returning home with bags of spiky prawns, Abbu set to work with rolled sleeves, a bucket of water and a bin. He knew that the next two hours would be filled with scrubbing, scraping and surgically removing the black spinal veins from the hunchbacked prawns. But his reward would be second helpings of this coastal dish, his taste buds petulantly disobeying the signals from his stomach that it was full. Platters brimming with fluffy pilau and rough chunks of lime upheld a steadfast Asian tradition of providing enough food to feed the neighbourhood. Bowls of thin chutney and crunchy lime-dressed salad coloured the dining table, and for a time the family would feel like members of a Mughal dynasty, for this was fine food. As Abbu swept his plate clean, he knew that this was how he wanted to live, with a simple, honest deliciousness.

PRAWN PILAU

Serves 4

450g basmati rice
2 tbsp olive oil
2 onions, finely sliced
3 garlic cloves, crushed
2 tsp cumin seeds
1 tsp fennel seeds
4cm fresh root ginger, peeled
4 green cardamom pods
1 tsp saffron strands

2 tsp garam masala (see page 46)
1 cinnamon quill
300ml boiling water
750g peeled cooked prawns
2 large tomatoes, chopped
1 lime, roughly chopped
Salt

Rinse the basmati rice a few times, drain and rest in a colander.

In a large lidded pan over a medium heat, fry 1 tbsp oil and cook half the onions, adding the garlic, cumin seeds and fennel seeds, and grating in the ginger. Sauté the ingredients until the ginger, onion and garlic have browned and the seeds fill the pan with toasted aromas: 3–4 minutes.

Add the cardamom pods, saffron strands, garam masala and cinnamon quill, pour in the boiling water and fold in the drained rice. Bring the pan to the boil, cover, reduce the heat to low and cook for 30 minutes, or until the rice is almost done. Add the cooked prawns and cook for 3–4 minutes until they've perked up and are pink, and the rice liquor is absorbed. Take off the heat.

In a separate pan, using the rest of the oil, fry the second onion until translucent, then slip in the tomatoes, cooking for 2 minutes until they've lost their form and become almost paste-like. Add these ingredients to the rice and stir through together with the lime.

Let the lime, fennel and creamy prawns delight your palate alongside fresh crunchy salad.

SWEET LIME WATER

Train stations across the Indian subcontinent play out similar scenes no matter where they are. Porters juggle luggage atop their wobbly heads as multitudes wearing sun-defying white shirts experience the smell of street food. Train announcers bleat through ageing speakers, squawking indecipherable destinations, and platforms teem with uni-formed train guards. Among all this, maimed beggars call out for a few pity rupees and hawkers offer hot chai and syrupy suet puddings.

These stations paint an accurate picture of urban life in towns across India and Pakistan: chaotic, overcrowded, hot, amusing, touching, and like nowhere else. Yet there was always one voice that managed to cut through the frequencies of the station. It was the call of the sweet-lime-water seller that captured Albert's attention as he boarded the train to visit his sister. The voice was always young, high-pitched and, like the nimbu pani (sweet lime water) on offer, there was a cheeky innocence to it that made him gladly part with a few rupees to gulp it down.

It's a simple concoction, and thirsty or not it's a treat worth discovering.

NIMBU PANI

Serves 4

75g sugar
750ml water
Juice of 2 limes

½ tsp salt
Crushed ice
Mint leaves

This thirst-buster takes no time at all. Mix the sugar and water until the sugar has completely dissolved, then add the lime juice and salt and stir until the water has turned cloudy. Now pour over crushed ice muddled with mint leaves. Sip and sigh with refreshment.

CAPITOL KEBABS

'You get the kebabs, I'll get the tea.'

That was the Friday pact between the teenage trio of Abbu and his best friends, Rocky and Samuel. With their smoothed hair and faces pricked by the early years of shaving, they would descend on the Iranian-run Café George and order a round of finely minced lamb seekh kebabs, knitted together with green chillies, coriander, onion and a distinctive 'George spice blend', accompanied with shallow dishes of sweetened mint and coriander chutney. The boys would tuck in to fuel their growing forms and slurp sweet milky tea from short, stout glasses. Café George was always busy. You didn't eat here because you were hungry, rather because it awoke an epicurean desire in all who graced its threshold. One ate here because the food was exquisite and it was the place to be seen. The kebab ritual always preceded the Friday matinee blockbuster at the Capitol Picture House, the finest cinema theatre in Karachi, where the three would join queues and part with their crumpled rupee notes in exchange for a slice of their Hollywood heroes: Jerry Lewis, Kirk Douglas, Charlton Heston and Burt Lancaster. Life seemed so simple back then. Money was earned and contributed to the family coffers and the rest was spent on good times, including visits to Café George to gorge on long shami kebabs – juicy, meaty and smooth-textured with plenty of dipping chutney. Perhaps the reason why Abbu is so fond of these meat treats is that they evoke the bygone era of his carefree youthful years when life was lived without the responsibility of adulthood.

SEEKH KEBABS

Serves at least 6 as a starter

3 small onions, chopped
6 garlic cloves, chopped
2 tsp cumin seeds
2 tsp fennel seeds
2 tbsp ginger paste
6 green chillies, 3 of them deseeded
Big bunch fresh coriander leaves
1 egg
1kg finely minced lamb
1 tbsp garam masala (see page 46)
1 tbsp ground coriander
Pinch of salt
Pinch of red chilli powder
4 tbsp gram (chickpea) flour

Using a blender, blitz the onion, garlic, cumin and fennel seeds, chillies and coriander leaves until the combination is finely minced, looking green and shot through with onion. Whisk an egg and set aside. In a large mixing bowl, massage the blended ingredients into the minced lamb, adding the garam masala, ginger paste, ground coriander, salt and red chilli powder. Once the ingredients are evenly combined, add in the flour and it will dry the combination a little. Now add the whisked egg as this will help cleave the ingredients together. Wrap the bowl in cling film and put in the fridge for 1 hour. Soak up to 12 bamboo skewers in water.

Take the chilled, marinated meat out of the fridge. Coat your hands in a little oil (stops the meat sticking to them) and shape Churchillian-sized cigars from the lamb around each skewer. They should have a firmish consistency.

Either BBQ, bake/grill or tandoor. All methods are straightforward, but if you barbecue make sure the coals are white hot and turn the kebabs regularly until they've taken on a slightly crispy appearance. If you bake/grill them, heat the oven to 200°C/Gas 6 and bake for 12–15 minutes, in an ovenproof tray, twisting them to baste on all sides, then brown under the grill on a medium heat for a few minutes until nicely bronzed. In a tandoor, hang and twist frequently for around 10 minutes.

Serve this Indian kebab with rings of onion fried in butter with a squish of lemon.

'IT'S JUST HOW I COOK'

'Brother, so sorry, it's gone ... we couldn't resist.'

Mrs Singh, the landlord's wife, offered Uncle Abbu an apologetic gesture, her painted eyebrows crinkled in her furrowed forehead as her lipstick-smudged teeth struggled to make an appearance in her thin guilty smile. Standing in the kitchen, Abbu looked beyond her broad sari'd frame and his eyes widened in disbelief. The pan he'd left on the top shelf from the night before was empty, wiped clean with the efficiency of soft, hot chapattis. He looked back at her and saw her fractured nail polish and her cuticles glowing yellow from the turmeric he'd used in the chicken he'd lovingly prepared the previous day.

It was this pot of promise that had got him through his twelve-hour shift working the looms at Brentford Nylons and assuaged his hunger and longing for home where his wife and children were, thousands of miles away in Karachi.

As Abbu returned Mrs Singh's pleading eyes with an expression of despair, she babbled to fill the silence. 'Brother' – the endearment didn't soften his tired expression – 'it was the smell, it became too much. We just tasted it and then little Rani wanted some and then ...' She shrugged her shoulders in submission. The curry had wrestled the entire family and their impromptu guests to the ground and satiated their desire. 'But I can buy some more chicken tomorrow and I'll cook,' she promised. Abbu's expression shifted to one of panic. Mrs Singh's cooking was so bad that even the birds avoided leftovers in the garden. Instead Abbu suggested he teach them to cook his 'stolen chicken'. Her head nodded as if detached from her body and Abbu resolved to console his loss with a pint and a mixed grill at the pub around the corner. The following evening, Najar Singh and his family crowded into the coffee-coloured kitchen and watched Abbu as he layered aromatics with spices and folded in yoghurt, dressing the chicken in a silky sheen as it combined with the oil. '*Achar*, so many spices, brother?' Lowering his tasting spoon, Abbu simply answered, 'It's just how I cook.'

STOLEN CHICKEN

Serves a hungry 4 or more

1kg chicken, either boneless or jointed
Sunflower oil
1 tsp coriander seeds
1 tsp cumin seeds
3 green cardamom pods
6 cloves
Salt
2 medium onions, chopped into tiny pieces
1 tbsp grated ginger
1 tbsp coarsely chopped garlic
2 medium tomatoes, chopped into small chunks
1 tsp garam masala (page 46)
Pepper
Fist of coriander leaves, to garnish

For the marinade

300g natural yoghurt, fork whipped and at room temperature
    (I like to use yoghurt with 10% fat)
Salt, to taste
¾ tsp turmeric powder
3 green finger chillies, chopped
1 tbsp olive oil

Mix all the ingredients for the marinade. Chop up or joint the chicken, coat it in the marinade and leave, covered, at room temperature for an hour (to prevent it from splitting when cooked).

In a large pan over a medium heat, theatrically glug in some oil and pop in the coriander and cumin seeds plus the cardamom, cloves, a little salt and the onions, frying until

the onions brown a little. Next, drop in the ginger and garlic and cook for approximately 5 minutes, stirring gently, then grind in the pepper, add the chopped tomatoes and garam masala, stirring for another 5 minutes or so until the mix is bubbling gently and on the verge of being a little sticky. Now it's time for the chicken to join the party (but hold back 2 tbsp of the yoghurt mix), so turn the heat up, add the pieces and fry on high for 3–4 minutes until the meat has turned from raw to white. Turn the heat down to low, cover and cook for a further 25 minutes, adding a little water to stop it from sticking. Check regularly, and fold in the rest of the yoghurt after 10 minutes. Keep an eye on this dish and make sure you stir it regularly to keep the yoghurt from splitting. Serve straight away (or keep for the next day where it tends to taste even better), garnished with coriander.

Ravish the chicken curry with rice or Chapattis (page 172). This is gorgeous with Frisco Zucchini (page 55).

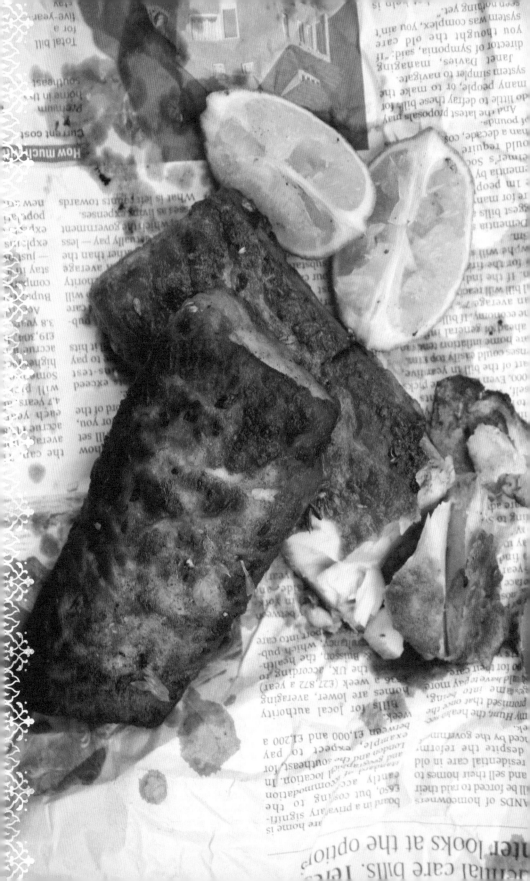

FISH AND CHIPS

'All right, Mike, we'll have two cod and chips and plenty of vinegar.'

In response, the white-aproned man raised a quizzical eyebrow at Rocky, who turned to Abbu for a clue. Having recently arrived in England, he was keen to embrace the fabric of British life and now his credibility was hanging by a thread.

'Salt with that?' enquired the owner.

'Thanks, Mike,' said Rocky with a wink, his confidence returned.

Abbu smirked at Rocky's eagerness and dropped the coins on to the counter in exchange for the parcels of greasy newspaper. Once outside, Abbu gave in to his suppressed laughter, slapping Rocky on the back with a free hand. 'Very good, Rock, very good.'

'*Achar*, what for?' he replied, keenly.

'"Mike?" What do you mean, "Mike"? Do you know him?'

'Well, that's what everybody says to each other: "All right, Mike?"'

Shaking his head and affectionately laughing at his friend's naivety, Abbu wondered whether to correct him or leave him to provide further amusement through his ignorance. He decided to spare his friend's embarrassment. '*Paaji* [brother], it's "mate" not "Mike" they're saying to each other.'

Rocky dipped his embarrassed face into the newspaper, hiding his flushed cheeks in the packet of steaming vinegary chips, quickly blowing to cool the lump of lava he'd just put into his mouth. With squeaky wooden forks they prised the fish into chunky white and gold pieces and savoured the nation's favourite dish. They walked silently, deciding whether they liked the tang of vinegar-soaked batter or not. Without looking up, Abbu muttered, 'Palla.' Rocky nodded his head and smiled, and for a moment they were back in a sun-soaked street in the Indian subcontinent picking the bones out of palla, fresh fried masala river fish. Their numbers swelled the Sindh river and fed the Sindhi population with its very own version of fish 'n' chips … no vinegar required.

SINDHI FISH FRY

Serves up to 8

8 white fish fillets, such as haddock,
     plaice or Vietnamese cobbler
1 tbsp turmeric powder
2 tbsp plain flour
1 tsp chilli powder
1 tbsp coriander seeds, bashed up
2 tsp fennel seeds, crushed
2 garlic cloves, crushed
2 tsp garam masala (see page 46)
1 tsp ground black pepper
Pinch of salt
Vegetable oil, enough to fry

Take a large plastic bag and pop in everything apart from
the fish and the oil. Give it a good shake to combine all the
dry ingredients. Now add one fillet at a time to the bag and
rhythmically rustle it, coating the fish in the masala mix.
Remove and do the same with the other fillets.

In a large frying pan, add enough vegetable oil to fry
the fish, approximately 5–7cm deep. Heat to a moderately
high temperature and test whether it's ready by dropping in
a small cube of bread. If the bread fizzes and turns brown
in 30 seconds, the oil is ready. Slip in a couple of fillets at a
time and cook for around 4–5 minutes, gently turning over
until it's turned a gorgeous golden yellow and almost ready to
flake. Drain on paper kitchen towels.

Serve with lime chunks and tear apart with your fingers.

BOND STORE BAKES

In 1976 Britain recorded its worst drought in history, Concorde took its first commercial flight and Steve Jobs formed Apple. It was also the year of the dream for Abbu as he finally joined British Airways, where he would spend the rest of his working life. He started off in the catering corps, working the night shift with a colony of immigrants doing the nocturnal work no one else wanted to do. It was here in the Bond Store that an alternative community flourished. Amongst the cases of Rémy Martin, Krug Champagne and bottles of Johnnie Walker Blue Label, a bazaar with all the trading bustle of the subcontinent sprang to life. Deals were shaken on for rent, card games were played on upturned crates, reggae music filled the air and Sikh luggage handlers traded electronics for whisky whilst the occasional Bond Store bursar turned a blind eye to missing inventory. All the while Abbu carefully counted out proud shiny miniatures of vodka, gin and whisky in exchange for tins and tubs of contraband food. Unwrapping the crinkled galaxy of tin foil, he released the head-turning scent of cloves, lemon, cumin and fat black cardamom pods. He inspected juicy pieces of tandoori chicken, crumbly vegetable pakoras and meaty lamb chappli kebabs, biting into one as if testing a gold nugget for its authenticity. The swap was only completed once the recipes accompanying these baked delights were produced. Looking over his shoulder as if to shield his illicit deal, Abbu released the miniatures as he sized up his hoard with Fagin-like fervour, stashing what he'd take home and grazing on the rest throughout his shift.

Bond Store bake treasures featured regularly at Abbu and Lorena's house parties, complemented by head-nodding reggae and shoulder-shrugging Bhangra. For me this is the soundtrack of immigration at work.

TANDOORI CHICKEN

Serves up to 20 as a side or starter

1kg chicken thighs or fillets, skinless
Juice of 1 lemon
Olive oil
Pinch of salt
3 fat garlic cloves, peeled
5cm fresh root ginger, peeled
300g natural yoghurt, fork whipped and at room temperature
   (I like to use yoghurt with 10% fat, but you can use low-fat
   if you like)
⅓ tsp cardamom powder
4 tsp paprika
2 tsp ground coriander
1 tsp garam masala (see page 46)
½ tsp chilli powder
½ tsp turmeric powder
½ tsp red food colouring (optional)
2 tsp cumin seeds, roughly ground
2 tsp fennel seeds, roughly ground

Slash the skinless chicken – if using fillets, cut into skewer-size
pieces – marinate in lemon juice, oil and salt, and refrigerate
for at least 1 hour. In the meantime, create the tandoori
marinade. Blitz the garlic in a blender with a little water to
create a paste, do the same with the ginger, and combine
with the yoghurt. Throw in all the other spices and mix well,
including the red food colouring. The marinade should take
on the hue of a prize-winning rose. I sometimes add in half a
sliced onion, if it's knocking around and needs using up. Add
the chilled chicken to the mix and thoroughly work it over as
if performing a Turkish massage on it, making sure all the

sauce is well and truly worked into the chicken. Cover and refrigerate for a couple of hours (or ideally overnight).

If using fillet pieces, skewer the chicken on to pre-soaked bamboo sticks. Cook under a hot grill for 20–25 minutes until the juices run clear when prodded. If cooking over coals in a tandoor or pizza oven it will take a similar amount of time. Again, prod the fattest piece with a fork and see if the juices run clear.

Serve with cool Raitha (page 224) or leave it naked with a few lemon wedges for comfort.

CHAPPLI KEBABS

Serves 6–8

6 tbsp freshly chopped coriander leaves
1 medium onion, chopped into large chunks
6 green chillies
10cm fresh root ginger, peeled and cut into chunks
1 tbsp coriander seeds, crushed
1 tsp cumin seeds
750g lamb or beef mince
1 tsp garam masala (see page 46)
3 tbsp gram (chickpea) flour
Salt
Vegetable oil, enough for shallow-frying (around 5mm depth
   in a frying pan)

These round 'sandal'-shaped minced lamb or beef kebabs are a popular barbecue snack. In a food processor, blend the coriander leaves, onion, chillies, ginger, and coriander and cumin seeds. In a large bowl, combine the mince, garam masala, flour and blended ingredients, and season with salt (reserve the oil). Get your hands stuck in and mix everything thoroughly.

Grease your hands with a little oil, tear off walnut-sized pieces and roll into balls. You should aim to have around 24. Now, with your thumb or the heel of your hand, gently flatten each ball, shaping them into an oval of around 2cm depth, until they look like the sole of a sandal, i.e. a chappal.

Over a medium heat, warm the oil in a large frying pan. Test if it's ready by tossing in a cumin seed – if the seed fizzes and swims it's good to go. Slide in a few kebabs at a time, cooking in a single layer for around 3–4 minutes on each side until browned.

Serve scorching hot with Sweet and Sour Tomato Chutney (page 87).

VEGETABLE PAKORAS

Serves at least 4

250g gram (chickpea) flour
50g self-raising flour
½ tsp cayenne pepper
1 tsp garam masala (see page 46)
Water to combine
300g potatoes, peeled and thinly sliced
½ cauliflower, sliced, then cut across into small chunks
1 tsp cumin seeds
12 spinach leaves, finely chopped
1 onion, finely sliced
1 tsp chopped green chilli
Bunch of coriander leaves
Pinch of salt
Sunflower oil, for deep frying

Sift both flours into a bowl, spoon in the cayenne pepper and garam masala and combine. Gradually add water, tablespoon by tablespoon, and work to form a batter smooth and thick enough to cling to the back of a spoon. Leave to rest for 15 minutes.

Apart from the oil, tip in the rest of the ingredients, making sure everything is coated. Pour enough sunflower oil in a deep frying pan or wok, and heat until a dropped cumin seed fizzes and swims. Carefully lower in tablespoons of the fritter mix. Work in batches, frying for approximately 3 minutes on each side until they've taken on the colour of caramel and the vegetables are cooked through, crispy and light.

Serve with a chutney of choice.

GOLDEN GHOBI

In many ways Abbu was living his dream. Having grafted to build a future for his family in Britain, he had finally realised his ambition of owning a house in West London which could accommodate his wife, four children and his elderly parents. Finally, after periods apart from each other, his family were united under one roof, having travelled from Pakistan at different times. Plus, he was now working for his beloved British Airways. However, all this came at a hefty price. With eight mouths to feed and a mortgage to pay, overtime on top of his lengthy shifts was a precious opportunity to make ends meet.

The weariness sat on his shoulders, reminding him of his childhood water-fetching days. Tiredness conquered every part of his body and he longed for the softness of his bed. Approaching the short path to the family home, his nose twitched like a rabbit's, sensing something in the air. It was unmistakable. Mama had been cooking and his heart soared. Although he was a family man, bearing the weight of his responsibilities, the smell delivered the comfort only a mother could give to a son. The house was yet to awake from its slumber and as he opened the door a scented tornado struck his senses, the distinct smell of roasted cumin and fennel seeds layered the air, followed by the honest earthiness of ghobi (cauliflower) and notes of garlic and chilli. Mama had prepared aloo ghobi. Some would refer to this dish as peasant food, but if peasants ate like this then surely they were the richest men of all.

Taking careful, quiet steps to the kitchen, he lifted the lid. He discovered a forest of ghobi gleaming richly as if it had been cooked in the juice of Bengali gold. Unfolding the checked tea towel, he revealed the chapattis, still breathing warm air. The golden ghobi crumbled into smaller florets and Abbu's hunger was beaten into submission by a dish created with a mother's pride.

ALOO GHOBI

Serves 4 as a side dish or 2 as a main

3 tbsp vegetable oil
½ tsp cumin seeds
1 tsp mustard seeds
Pinch of asafoetida (optional)
2 green chillies, finely chopped
3 medium potatoes, cut into smallish cubes
1 medium cauliflower, trimmed and cut into bite-size florets
75ml water
1 tsp salt
Half a lemon

For the spice paste

2.5cm fresh root ginger, peeled and blended to make a paste
    with 2 tbsp water
1 tbsp ground coriander
¼ tsp turmeric powder
1 tsp curry powder
4 tbsp water

Combine all the spice paste ingredients in a bowl.

Heat the oil over a medium heat and test the heat by torturing a single cumin seed. If it fizzes and pops then the oil is ready. Add the rest of the cumin, the mustard seeds, asafoetida (if you have some) and chillies, stirring for just a few seconds. Now add the spice mix and stir for a minute or two until the mix separates a little from the oil. Slide in the potatoes (aloo) and cauliflower (ghobi), adding the water and salt, and mix well, covering everything with everything. Cover and cook over a medium heat for 15–20 minutes until the vegetables have yielded their starchy stiffness and become tender and submissive. Check the aloo ghobi during this time and, if it's sticking to the pan, add a touch more water. Just before serving, squish the juice of half a lemon over the aloo ghobi and mix well, making sure you don't crush the contents.

Tear into this recipe armed only with fresh flatbread.

MUSTARD AND SPINACH LEAVES

Saag is the name for the leaves of the mustard plant, but as they were not readily available in England they were often replaced by spinach leaves (palak), which by proxy became known as saag. Saag aloo was often cooked for my uncle Abbu by my grandmother, and I like her technique of using floury potatoes in this dish as they soak up the spices when squashed with a chapatti scoop of saag.

SAAG ALOO

Serves 2 as a main or 4 as a side dish

1 tbsp vegetable oil
1 tsp cumin seeds
1 onion, sliced
2 garlic cloves, finely chopped
2 green chillies, finely chopped
4cm fresh root ginger, peeled
1 tsp ground cumin
1 tsp ground coriander
50ml water
4 medium potatoes, peeled and diced into bite-sized chunks
240g tinned spinach with its juices
½ tsp garam masala (see page 46)
Salt

Using a frying pan, heat the oil to a medium temperature and fry the cumin seeds until they start sizzling, then add the onion, cooking until translucent. Pop in the garlic and chillies and grate in the ginger. Don't let the ingredients stick to the pan. As soon as it starts to brown, introduce the ground cumin and coriander. Stir and cover everything with the powdered spices – the ingredients will dry up a little so add the water and potatoes, cooking for 3–4 minutes until they become opaque.

Now the hard part … add the tinned spinach and all its juices. Stir regularly and lower the heat, cooking for 10–12 minutes until the potatoes have started to crumble around the edges or you can pierce a chunk with a fork. Spoon in the garam masala and salt to taste, mix thoroughly and simmer for a couple more minutes. The potatoes should be crumbly, yellow and peeping through the dark green mere.

WASTE NOT, WANT NOT

With a number of mouths to feed, Uncle Abbu and Auntie Lorena often found they had a mix of vegetables left by the end of the week. Never wasting a scrap of food, Abbu would use them up, giving them a fitting end to their purpose. Taking the motley crew of peas, carrots, tomatoes, potatoes, onions and any other vegetable looking forlorn and lonely, he'd create a quick, tasty fricassee of spiced mixed sabzi. It was healthy, easy to digest and brightened up by as many chillies as one could tolerate.

This dish is cracking with a chunky helping of lime pickle.

MIXED SABZI

Serves 4

4 medium carrots, peeled and
  chopped into batons
200g green beans, chopped
  into 2cm lengths
2 large potatoes, peeled and
  diced
2 peppers, whatever colour
  you prefer, chopped
3 tbsp vegetable oil
1 tsp cumin seeds
2 onions, roughly chopped
1 green chilli, chopped
⅓ tsp turmeric powder

2 tsp garlic paste (page 93)
2 tsp ginger paste (page 93)
2 tomatoes, finely chopped
100g tomato purée
1 tsp garam masala
1 tsp ground coriander
½ tsp cayenne pepper
½ tsp sugar
Salt, to taste
150ml water
2 tbsp fresh coriander leaves
Squeeze of fresh lemon

Steam the carrots, beans, potatoes and peppers for 6 minutes
until the vegetables have become al dente. In a large frying
pan, heat the oil over a medium temperature and fry the cumin seeds until they splutter. Now drop in the onions, chilli,
turmeric powder, ginger and garlic paste, and sauté until the
onions become opaque. Add the tomatoes and purée, garam
masala, ground coriander, cayenne pepper, sugar and salt,
and stir well. Add 100ml water, turn the heat to low and
cook for 5 minutes until the consistency has thickened. Now
introduce the vegetables to the pan, add the remaining water
and cook for 10 minutes or until the potatoes have softened,
the sauce is clinging to the sabzi and the oil has risen to the
surface of the vegetables.

Sprinkle with coriander leaves and squish a lemon over
this dish just before serving.

THE GURU SERIES

Asian families are like Agatha Christie novels – they go on for ever. This is mainly because they consist of friends of the family who become family members, i.e. 'uncles' and 'aunties'. They become 'family' from the moment they can pinch your cheeks in a vice-like grip between thumb and forefinger, whilst your parents urge you to smile through the ordeal. Uncle 'this' and Auntie 'that' earn their status through being a friend of the family. However, some earn a special place in our hearts. This was the case with the flamboyant Uncle Ikram, a Pakistani version of Woody Allen, and his wonderfully talented wife, Auntie Najma, whose prowess in the kitchen gave her licence to tweak my cheeks at will. Visiting their house was like going to the circus. Uncle Ikram would act out the ringmaster role with theatrical aplomb – upturned hands and a slap on the back preceded with 'Oh ho, guru!' loosely translated as 'All right, chief?', which he'd reserve for male members of the family. As children, we'd master the fine art of competing on the carom board while the women caught up on missed gossip and the fellas reminisced by telling the same old jokes and stories, often led by Uncle Ikram. The smell and sight of dish after dish of the most exquisite spiced food would turn even the most virtuous diner into a fiendish glutton, and while the memories carry a 1970s sepia tone, the food is as vivid now as it was then. Auntie Najma and Uncle Ikram's kitchen knowhow from their days as chefs in Pakistan was never fully revealed, and my father and his brother's attempts at curry reproduction never came close, apart from Uncle Abbu's. To date his interpretations of Auntie Najma's curried splendour are the best in the family … just don't tell the others.

CHICKEN BHUNA

Serves 4

125ml olive oil
2 medium onions, finely chopped
4 garlic cloves, crushed
3 green chillies, finely sliced
1 tsp crushed coriander seeds
1 tsp cayenne pepper
1 tbsp ground coriander
½ tsp turmeric powder
200ml water
6 chicken breasts, skinless, boneless, cut into large cubes
3 large tomatoes, chopped
1 tsp ground ginger
1½ tsp garam masala (see page 46)
3 tbsp chopped coriander leaves
Salt

Unlike the creamy, timid versions found in most Indian restaurants, this chicken bhuna is packed with vigour, depth and assertiveness.

In a large wok or frying pan, heat half the oil over a medium temperature and sauté the onions and garlic until soft. Add the chillies, coriander seeds, cayenne pepper, ground coriander and turmeric and stir for a couple of minutes, then add the water to create a paste. Turn the heat to high and cook for 2 minutes, then add the chicken chunks and turn down the heat to low, season with salt and simmer for 10–15 minutes until the chicken is part cooked. Put in the tomatoes, ground ginger and turn up to a medium heat. Stir and keep a watchful eye, cooking for 5 minutes until the sauce has reduced and the tomatoes are more like a purée.

Add the rest of the olive oil, stirring well to make sure the ingredients don't stick, if needs be adding a touch more water. Cook, stirring, for another 5 minutes or until you notice the oil rising to the surface and the gravy has become a little thicker. Sprinkle in the garam masala, stir well and scatter with coriander leaves.

It's ready to dish up with a side of ghobi (Cauliflower, see page 158) and naans.

MASALA GHOSHT

Serves 4

300ml natural yoghurt, at room temperature (I like to use one
    with 10% fat but you can use low-fat yoghurt if you like)
Generous handful of coriander leaves, chopped
4 green chillies, finely chopped
½ tsp turmeric powder
Pinch of salt
60ml sunflower oil
8 green cardamom pods
4 black cardamom pods
6 cloves
1 cinnamon quill
12 curry leaves
3 bay leaves
10 black peppercorns
1 tsp fennel seeds
1 tsp coriander seeds
½ onion, finely chopped
500g lamb, cut into chunks
6 garlic cloves, crushed
6cm fresh root ginger, peeled and chopped into matchsticks
150ml water

The intensity of this dish lies in the whole spices, fried in the
pan together with the lamb. The spices take on a different
aromatic structure and transform the dish into something
altogether richer and deeper. Apart from turmeric, there are
no ground spices at work, leaving you with the unadulterated
taste of whole spices.

    Step 1: Take the yoghurt, chopped coriander leaves, chil-
lies, turmeric and salt and mix well. Leave to stand.

Step 2: Heat the oil in a large pan over a medium temperature and add the cardamoms, cloves, cinnamon quill, curry and bay leaves, peppercorns, fennel and coriander seeds and fry for just under a minute until they've darkened in colour and they acquiesce their aroma. Add the onion, lamb, garlic and ginger and brown for 5–6 minutes.

Step 3: Take the pan from the heat, tip in the yoghurt mix, stir well, then return to the heat and cook for another 3–4 minutes. The oil should separate. Pour in the water, combine vigorously and turn up the heat until the pan is bubbling. Turn down to a low heat and leave to simmer for up to 2 hours or until the lamb has become tender and easy to tear apart with a fork.

Serve with rice and the cauliflower dish that follows, or try it with Tollywood Vegetables (page 210).

CAULIFLOWER WITH A TEMPER

Serves 4 as a side

3 tbsp vegetable oil
1 tsp fennel seeds
1 cinnamon quill
2 green cardamom pods
4 cloves
2 onions, finely chopped
2 tsp ginger paste (see page 93)
2 tsp garlic paste (see page 93)
2 fat tomatoes, chopped

Pinch of salt
½ tsp garam masala (see page 46)
½ tsp cayenne pepper
1 tbsp ground coriander
Pinch of asafoetida or mango powder
50ml water
1 cauliflower, florets cut into bite-size pieces
½ lemon

Cauliflower rarely tasted so delicious as when prepared by the hands of Uncle Ikram, with florets coated in tangy tomatoes, tempered spices releasing notes of aniseed and rich warming cinnamon ready to crumble on the tongue.

To make the spice temper, heat the oil in a large lidded pan over a medium temperature and tip in the fennel seeds, cinnamon, cardamom and cloves. Allow to darken for a minute or two, then add the onions, frying until opaque. Stir in the ginger and garlic pastes, cooking for 2 minutes, then introduce the tomatoes and salt. Fry the mix for 3–4 minutes or until the tomatoes give in and become maudlin. Sprinkle in the garam masala, cayenne pepper, ground coriander and asafoetida/mango powder, stir and cook for 4 minutes. Pour in the water and stir to create a loose paste, then lower the heat, pop in the cauliflower florets, cover and simmer for 10 minutes or until you can pierce a fork into the thickest floret.

Squeeze the lemon over the cauliflower and serve with Chicken Bhuna (page 166) or Masala Ghosht (pages 168).

THE TASTE OF CENTURIES

The earliest memory I have of eating Indian food is the smell of freshly cooked chapattis – round placemat-sized discs of blistered, unleavened bread straight from the cast-iron tawa, glistening with the sheen of butter, piping hot and passing the taste of centuries across my tongue. My method of cooking chapattis remains largely unchanged and this ancient bread that is flick-flacked between palms and made from the simplest ingredients still incites giddy waves of excitement within me. They're used instead of a knife and fork or chopsticks and are a far tastier instrument to gobble food with. Whether the curry is runny or dry, the occasion is never complete without them. This nostalgic introduction to home cooking is of course shared by millions, not least my uncle Abbu. Like me he watched his mother shape the flattened floured rounds of dough and smelt the bread cooking on a tawa before it was devoured by a hungry pack of siblings. However, in his household, chapatti making is shrouded in mystery. Some assert Auntie Lorena is the chief chapatti steward, but Uncle Abbu claims otherwise. All I know is that the kitchen door is shut as they're being made, and when it's opened a swell of fresh bread and melting butter sweeps your hunger into overdrive.

CHAPATTIS

Makes at least 8–10 chapattis

450g chapatti flour (You should be able to get your hands on
chapatti flour in most supermarkets. If not, mix equal
amounts of plain white and wholemeal flour.)
250ml water
Pinch of salt
Glug of olive oil
Butter to spread on top

Taking a large bowl, mix the flour, water, salt and oil to make
a dough, working it over with your knuckles and balls of your
palms for a soft, pliable consistency. The mix shouldn't be
too wet and sticky. If it is, dust with a little extra flour until it
is pliable and soft. Cover the bowl and pop in the fridge for
30 minutes.

Using a tawa or a largish frying pan, set it over a medium-
high heat. Now knead the dough and dust with some more
flour if it's still too sticky. Tear off onion-sized lumps – you
should get about 8–10. Place on a floured surface, keeping
them covered with a damp cloth. Gently flatten a ball of
dough and roll out into a disc of some 12cm in diameter.
Like a pizza base, flick-flack it between your palms to knock
some of the flour dust off and place it on the pan. Using
a tea towel as a dabber, gently press on the chapatti to
ensure it's being cooked through. You're using the tea towel
to press around the edges, making sure the thickest part
of the chapatti gets cooked. Let it cook for 10 seconds or
so, then flip over, repeating the process twice more or until
you see patches of warm brown scalding and puffed-up hot
air pockets. It's ready. Our family uses a tea towel-wrapped
plate to host the chapattis. Unfold the tea towel, pop the

chapatti on the plate and cover it with the other half of the towel. Cook the rest of the chapattis, spread one side with butter and then scoop up your chosen curry with your fresh chapattis and allow happiness to enter your soul.

GOOD FOOD KARMA

Some things in life are synonymous with each other. They complete the picture or the expected persona, like the Queen and her corgis or Britain and the rain. The same can be said for spiced food. Regardless of whether it's Indian dishes, Middle Eastern mezzes or Mexican chipotle recipes – they need their salsa, relishes, raithas and chutneys. Call it good food karma.

There's rarely an occasion where Uncle Abbu's dinner table isn't graced with a raitha, dahi (yoghurt-based dip) or chutney. This is one of the more popular ones, often spooned alongside rice dishes or dry spiced chicken starters.

CORIANDER CHUTNEY

Makes enough to accompany the kebab or pakora recipes

50g fresh coriander leaves, rinsed and roughly picked from the stalks
2 garlic cloves, peeled
2 green chillies
1 tbsp lemon juice
2 tbsp water
200ml natural yoghurt, fork whipped and at room temperature (I like to use yoghurt with 10% fat)
½ tsp salt
½ tsp sugar

In a blender blitz the coriander, garlic, chillies, lemon juice and water. Pulse everything for a minute. Tip the contents into a bowl containing the yoghurt and mix thoroughly with the salt and sugar. If it needs a little more seasoning, then add according to your taste.

INDIAN RICE PUDDING

Rice pudding is a perennial favourite, following us throughout life. Some childhood memories invoke thoughts of a sweet crust concealing delicious, piping-hot creamed rice, but in the case of my school dinners what I actually remember is a congealed mass of bloated bumps. Some assert that India was the birthplace of rice pudding. True or not, kheer is the most refined form of rice as a dessert. It is aristocratic and delicate, touched by the magic of cardamom dust and blessed with whole milk.

Over the years as I watched Uncle Abbu luxuriate in each spoonful of kheer, pudding envy set in. He'd discovered the joy of kheer long before I had, and he'd not had to endure the porridge of wallpaper paste set before me in the school canteen. So before baking yet another regular rice pudding, try its more elegant ancestor. Once tasted you'll make sure it's kheer to stay.

KHEER

Serves 4

2 litres whole milk
60g plain white rice, soaked for 10 minutes then rinsed
2 tbsp cornflour
160g unrefined sugar
5 green cardamom pods, seeds extracted and pounded into
   powder
2 tbsp crushed almonds and pistachios, for garnishing

Using a large pan, heat the milk (reserving 3–4 tbsp for later) until bubbling but not boiling, then reduce the heat and add the rice. Simmer for 20 minutes until the rice has soaked in the milk and broken down. In a separate bowl, mix the cornflour and the reserved milk into a paste. Add the paste to the simmering rice and stir well, not letting any lumps form, and keep stirring until it thickens. Spoon in the sugar and cardamom dust and bring to the boil. Once bubbling, take off the heat and leave the kheer to relax. Dish out into small bowls and sprinkle the surface with the crushed nuts.

ONE-POT WONDER

'Your uncle's been cooking.'

The glee in my auntie Lorena's voice reflected the joy of her taste buds. Although a superb cook herself, she adores my uncle Albert's kitchen know-how. Together they've experienced the vigour and rigour of immigration and fed countless party guests and family members. Throughout this there's one thing that remains consistent – whatever the time of day, there's always a pot of something on the stove. It could be as simple as everyday daal, aloo ghobi or a silky chicken recipe. However, there's one dish that's a staple favourite, and its earthy, warm, home-coming smell tells a story of lamb that has been braised with smashed spices, allowing its nutritious bone juice to flavour the citrusy coriander seeds and temper the fight in the green chillies. The late addition of tinned spinach leaves (try not to be a food snob here – I've tried it with fresh leaves and the tins produce a warmer result), left to simmer, delivers a hotpot that needs no other accompaniment other than some flatbread.

This recipe's roots lie in the meat-eating Punjab. It's a handy number to try out as it'll keep for a couple of days, providing sustenance for impromptu guests or employed simply to satisfy the demands of a hungry family.

PUNJABI HOTPOT

Serves 4–6

4 tbsp vegetable oil
1kg lean lamb, some on the
    bone, cut into 4cm chunks
    (you can use boneless lamb
    but I think meat on the
    bone is far tastier)
2 medium onions, chopped
4 garlic cloves, crushed
3 green chillies, chopped
6cm fresh root ginger, peeled
2 tsp ground cumin

1 tbsp ground coriander
1 tbsp paprika
1 tsp turmeric powder
400g tinned tomatoes
350ml water
240g tinned spinach
2 tsp garam masala (see
    page 46)
Big bunch of fresh coriander
Salt

Using a large pan, heat 2 tbsp oil to a medium-high temperature and brown the lamb all over. It should relinquish some nice meaty juices. Remove the meat, add the remaining oil to the pan and sauté the onions until brown. Add the garlic and chillies and grate in the ginger, then stir in the cumin, coriander, paprika and turmeric, and fry for 3–4 minutes. Pour in the tomatoes and pop in the meat along with the water and season with salt. Turn up the heat and bring to the boil for a couple of minute. Reduce the heat, cover and simmer for 1½ hours or until the meat is succulently tender. Tip in the spinach and garam masala and cook for a further 10 minutes.

    Serve with a flourish of coriander.

SALAD TRICOLOUR

This salad is a regular at our dinner table, sitting ringside to the other dishes as a refreshing, tart antidote to thundery spices. It harmonises the voices of a few simple ingredients: red onions, portly tomatoes, sharp vinegar, youthful lemons and leafy coriander. If there's a bunch of us we'll plate this salad up on a platter, layering ingredients over each other. Otherwise we'll finger-mix the sliced ingredients in a bowl. Don't make this salad too far in advance of eating as the ingredients will lose their vitality. I call it Desi (Indian) Salad.

DESI SALAD

Serves 4 as a side

4 fat ripe tomatoes
1 red onion
Fist of torn coriander leaves
Juice of half a lemon
20ml white wine vinegar
Olive oil
Salt flakes

Slice up the tomatoes and red onion, sprinkle with coriander and layer over each other on a platter. Douse with the lemon juice, spritz with vinegar and glug with enough oil to glisten the surface. Pepper with salt flakes. Leave to stand for 10 minutes.

SWEET ASPIRATIONS

Each grain of rice shone spectacularly, carefully painted by the luminescent saffron. Speckled with the colours of a tutti-frutti ice cream, fat raisins and plump pistachios twinkled, echoing the disco lights which now moved in time with the bhangra beats of my cousin Reba's wedding to her Indian fiancé Ricky. As she was Uncle Albert's eldest daughter, the extravagance knew no bounds. The sweet rice served in celebration of their nuptials reflected the moment perfectly. Curvy women spilling from their saris shook and shrugged to the thumping beats clad in eye-poppingly bright silk, moustachioed husbands rolled their torsos in time, whilst younger, more athletic males leapt on to shoulders to add height to the throng. The blur of smiles, colour and fierce bhangra activity perfectly describes the mood of zarda.

For Abbu perhaps the dish served as a metaphor, a moment of utter contentment, seeing his offspring married and settled in the country of his aspiration. A sweet recipe for all concerned.

ZARDA

Serves 14 or more … well, it is made for parties

750g white rice
1 litre water
¼ tsp yellow food colouring
12 green cardamom pods
2 tbsp vegetable oil
400g unrefined sugar
2 tbsp double cream
2 tbsp raisins
1 tbsp pistachios, gently crushed
2 tsp orange zest
1 tbsp almonds, flaked

Rinse the rice, two or three times. Using a large pot, boil the water with the food colouring and drop in half the cardamom pods. Pour in the rice, reduce the heat and simmer for 20 minutes. Drain the rice and set aside.

Using a large lidded pan, heat the oil over a low heat and fry the remaining cardamom pods for a couple of minutes. Tip in the rice and sugar, stir, cover and cook for 5 minutes. Stir a couple of times to make sure it doesn't stick to the pan. Take the rice off the heat and stir in the cream, raisins, pistachios, orange zest and almonds.

Spoon into small bowls and let the party continue.

PART FOUR
LAWRIE UNCLE
(UNCLE LAWRENCE)

LAWRENCE PETERS

The skinny man wearing headphones simply nodded his head and bellowed, 'Action!' The command sprang the beautiful people into life, cameras whirred and the actors pretended the crew weren't there as they spun through their lines.

Leaning on a friend's shoulder, Lawrie was transfixed by the activity. He was watching from the position of a hill looking down into a valley, and it was there he observed that the real power was behind the camera, not in front of it. He decided there and then – his fate was sealed. He would be in the movie business.

As a child, being the second youngest he often scored treats from his elder siblings, and his favourite was a trip to the flicks. He would sit with his hands cradling his cherubic round face, fingers digging into his puppy-fat cheeks. His ferocious, high-pitched laugh sent infectious ripples throughout the cinema, causing shoulders to shrug as he giggled away obliviously. His raven black, wavy hair and eyes wide with wonder combined in a look he has managed to carry throughout his life. With his slight vulnerability, charm and lexicon of jokes, he's worked hard at being happy-go-lucky.

Lawrie achieved his dream by joining the popular Eastern Studios as an apprentice sound recordist. He quickly became a mascot of popularity, sprinkling charm in his wake, drawing affection from all those he worked with and gaining a particularly strong

Jan Mayen
(Nor.)
North Cape
NORWEGIAN
SEA
Faeröerne
(Den.)
Oslo
Glasgow
North
Sea
London
Paris
FRANCE
Madrid
SPAIN
Rome
ITALY
Mediterranean
Sea
Warsaw
Kharkov
Stalingrad
YUGO
BUL.
Black
Sea
Caspian
Sea
Baku
Aral Sea
Tashkent
Istanbul
TURKEY
SYRIA
IRAQ
Tehran
IRAN
AFGH.
Kabul
PAK
Karachi
New
Delhi
ISR
Cairo
EGYPT
Nile
Red Sea
SAUDI
ARABIA
Mecca
OMAN
(Br.)
ADEN
ARABIAN
SEA
G. of Aden
Bombay
GÔA
(Port.)
CEYLON
Algiers
TUNISIA
(Fr.)
Tripoli
ALGERIA
(Fr.)
LIBYA
S A H A R A
FR. W. AFRICA
A F R I C A
(Br.)
NIGERIA
Lagos
GOLD
COAST
FR.
EQUAT.
AFRICA
ANGLO-
EGYPTIAN
SUDAN
Addis Ababa
ETHIOPIA
SOM'LD.
Mogadiscio
UGANDA
KENYA
(Br.)
Nairobi
BELG.
Brazzaville
Léopoldville
CONGO
TANGANYIKA
Dar es Salaam
Seychelles
(Br.)
Luanda
ANGOLA
(Port.)
FED.
OF RH.
& NY.
MOZAMBIQUE (Port.)
Mozambique
Chan.
MADAGASCAR
(Fr.)
Mauritius (Br.)
Reunion
(Fr.)
I N D I A N
S. W.
AFRICA
Windhoek
BECH.
Johannesburg
U. OF
SO. AFR.
Lourenço
Marques
Capetown
C. of Good Hope
Omsk
Kiev

female following. Love blossomed early and, like in the movies, he got the girl he'd hoped for, marrying his sweetheart, Loelly, at the age of twenty. Theirs was a carefree, youthful union, the two of them against the world. Their love brought a wonderful little boy, yet tragedy lurked in the shadows of their joy and Loelly was robbed of a maternal life. She died, leaving behind a newborn son and a heartbroken husband. Lawrie's fragile state left him with no option but to have the boy adopted by another family member to give him the best start in life. He threw himself into work and rose through the ranks, working with the industry's big-name film directors, eating on the go, looking for fulfilment and opportunities to fill his time and discover his big break. Eventually *it* found *him*. A delegation from the United Arab Emirates was looking for a crew to make a film on the Arab states. Lawrie was in, and adventure, money and travel took him to Abu Dhabi. It was here that he found his culinary voice, sharing digs with a melting pot of subcontinent cousins – Punjabis, Gujarathis, Sindhis and Parsis. His appetite for cooking grew alongside his curiosity for regional dishes. Exchanging recipes, he traded dishes from his youth – Siberian duck curry, lamb bhuna, shaljam ghosht – and in turn his repertoire extended to accommodate the diversity of his new companions.

But Lawrie's spirit was drawn towards his family who were now in England and, despite protestations from friends, at the age of forty he left the film business and once more embarked on the immigrant trail.

As the last of his brothers to arrive in England, he was always busy chasing jobs and finding love – both of which he managed with varying degrees of success. Flighty is a good description of his life and his food. His preference is for quick cooking, taking short-cuts without sacrificing taste. Sometimes poetic, occasionally melancholic, his cooking carries a happy-go-lucky rhythm, flavoured by three continents.

THE TASTE OF HAPPINESS

Seventy kilometres north of Karachi lies a body of water known as Haleji Lake, which was expanded during World War II to accommodate the needs of Allied soldiers. During the winter the lake operates as an oasis and rest stop for ducks migrating from Siberia, escaping the harsh months ahead. Man-sized rushes fringing the lake also provide perfect cover for lone hunters, who present their spoils in the covered markets in Karachi. The journey for these feathered friends finishes in the home kitchens of this ocean city and, in the past, at the dextrous fingers of Mama Peters, who would massage these birds with masala-rich fingers and create a game curry of noble proportions. This recipe was one to be revered, honoured and eaten with aplomb. Lawrie's demeanour would change when eating it. He'd adopt a regal approach to this fine dining dish, throwing back his shoulders and stiffening his back – assuming the position of someone several stations above his born status. The tender birds would fall apart in the rich cardamom and cinnamon gravy, and as he tucked each morsel into his mouth he knew that he'd tasted happiness.

SIBERIAN DUCK CURRY

Serves 4

120ml vegetable oil
2.5–3kg duck, jointed and cut into about 8 pieces
6 fat black cardamom pods
1 cinnamon quill
2 medium onions, sliced finely
3 fresh green chillies, finely sliced
4 garlic cloves, smashed
6cm fresh root ginger, peeled and finely chopped
1 tbsp ground coriander
½ tsp chilli powder
1 tbsp ground cumin
3 very ripe tomatoes, chopped
500ml water
Salt
¾ tsp ground cinnamon
2 tsp garam masala (see page 46)
20 fresh curry leaves

Using a large lidded pan, warm the oil over a medium heat and pop in all the duck pieces, skin-side down, leaving them to sizzle for a couple of minutes on each side, browning the duck fully. Take the duck out and set aside.

Using the same oil, slide in the cardamom pods, cinnamon quill and onions, cooking until the onions tan, then quickly add in the chillies, garlic and ginger and fry for another minute. Sprinkle in the coriander, chilli and cumin and stir for 1 minute, allowing the powders to soak up some of the juices. Next, introduce the tomatoes, allowing them to hiss and relax into a puréed state for 2 minutes. Don't let them burn. Return the duck to the pan and pour in the water and curry leaves, arouse all the ingredients and bring to the boil, then reduce to a low heat, cover and simmer for 80 minutes. You'll need to check on the duck's state and stir the dish every now and then.

Add a dash of salt, then scatter the cinnamon into the mix. Stir well and cook for another 15 minutes or until the duck is ready to fall apart. The duck may relinquish fat, which will rise to the surface. Tip the pan and spoon off the excess fat. As with most meat-based curries, they taste better the next day. So if you can, cook it the night before, refrigerate and then heat through.

Best enjoyed with rice and a Desi Salad (page 181).

DAY-DREAMER

Oblivious to the world around him, little Lawrie sat on the doorstep, knees propping up his elbows whilst his pudgy fingers cradled his face. As he looked out on the world beyond the family home his mind was far from reality. He was indulging in his favourite pastime instead: day-dreaming about his silver-screen heroes and the glamour of the movie theatre. One day he'd be rubbing shoulders with the star directors behind these epics and taste the energy of a film set. For now the dream remained exactly that. His imagination gradually drifted back to reality, pulled back in part by the nutty spiced smell of chick peas roasting in an open pan, waltzing with the sharp juices of tomatoes, attracting the attention of glistening onions and dry spices desperate to join the gathering. He felt the familiar experience of a grumbling stomach and heard the call from his father to join the family. Both commands were to be obeyed at all times. Tasting the little musket balls drenched in masala, it's no wonder that hesitation never featured in Lawrie Uncle's diet.

CHANNA MASALA

Serves 4 as a side

3 tbsp vegetable oil

1 medium onion, finely chopped

1 tbsp garlic paste (see page 93)

1 tbsp ginger paste (see page 93)

120ml water

2 green chillies, finely sliced

½ tsp turmeric powder

½ tsp cayenne pepper

1 tsp ground coriander

2 medium tomatoes, chopped

400g tin of boiled chickpeas

1 tsp salt

1 tsp garam masala (see page 46)

2 tbsp chopped coriander leaves

Over a medium heat, warm the oil in a large saucepan, tip in the onion, garlic and ginger pastes, and gently sauté until the ingredients tan. Use a little of the water to stop the mixture sticking. Add the green chillies, turmeric, cayenne pepper, ground coriander and a little more of the water, stirring until the ingredients have created the beginnings of spice paste. Pop in the tomatoes and turn to a low heat, cook for about 8 minutes until the tomatoes and friends have mingled and formed a bubbling purée. Christen with some more of the water to keep the consistency from drying out. Now introduce the chickpeas and the rest of the water and stir well, making sure the chickpeas are wearing a spice coat. Cover and cook for 15 minutes, until the chickpeas have absorbed most of the sauce and the oil is glistening. Stir in the garam masala and flutter with coriander.

Serve with flatbread and a chutney of choice. This is divine with Kismet Korma (page 112).

THE ONE THAT GOT AWAY

Family chores were plentiful in the Peters household, in part because of the size of the clan. Water needed to be pumped and carried, yards had to be swept, washing had to be done, food had to be collected, vegetables required tending and harvesting, and chickens needed to be fed and protected. This last duty was the bane of Lawrie's younger years – the thought of shepherding the clucking, squawking, scratching, feathered food into the chicken coop filled him with dread. He knew the chickens had it in for him. Determined to degrade his dignity, they wouldn't stop flapping, running and shrieking as he tried to catch them, his thick-set frame darting hither and thither. They kicked dust in his face and he was convinced they were mocking him. His black wavy hair was slicked by the sweat of his exertion as he counted them into the coop. '… eight, nine, ten, eleven, twel— where's the twelfth?' On the other side of the fence he could hear the solitary clucking cackle of the one that got away. As he squinted into the sun and smeared the sweat out of his eyes, he caught the silhouette of the strutting chicken heading off to new pastures. A cheer went up from the coop – the rest of the brood had created a diversion, giving number twelve an opportunity to perform a great escape. Horror gripped Lawrie by the buttock cheeks, as he knew for certain that they'd meet the wrath of his mother's slipper if he lost a precious chicken. He resorted to a natural instinct – story-telling – and created a tale of impressive eloquence, involving shape-shifting chicken rustlers and his heroic efforts to foil them. Nodding patiently, my grandmother gently reached for the slipper. Tall stories didn't entertain her. In homage to the one that got away, here are three recipes she narrowly escaped: kebab, followed by slow-cooked biryani (page 198), with its layers of spiced and coloured rice, and a silky dish that uses the earthiness of fenugreek leaves (methi).

CHICKEN RUSTLER KEBAB

Serves 4 as an appetiser

1 large onion, roughly chopped
Bunch of coriander leaves
1 tbsp fennel seeds
4 green chillies, chopped
120ml natural yoghurt, at room temperature (I like to use one with 10% fat)
100ml single cream
½ tsp clove powder
½ tsp ground mace
1 tbsp garlic paste (see page 93)
1 tbsp ginger paste (see page 93)
Salt and pepper
750g chicken breast, sliced into skewer-sized chunks
Lemon

In a blender, attack the onion, coriander leaves, fennel seeds and chillies. In a bowl, combine the yoghurt, cream, clove, mace, garlic and ginger pastes. Season with salt and a twist of pepper. Tip in the blended ingredients and mix thoroughly.

Score the chicken breast chunks and baptise them in the marinade. Cover and refrigerate for 2 hours. Thread on to metal skewers or soaked bamboo ones. Keep the marinade for further basting.

Over hot barbecue coals or under a preheated grill set to a medium heat, roast for 8–10 minutes, rotating regularly. Baste with some more of the marinade and grill for another 4 minutes or until cooked. The chicken should have a firm springiness. Spritz with the juice of a lemon just before serving.

Serve with a dipping chutney of choice and a side of Kachumbar (page 35). This is also great alongside California Cabbage Sizzle (page 58).

CHICKEN BIRYANI

Serves up to 6

150ml vegetable oil (it's a fair amount of oil but you need it to create lots of silky gravy)

4 onions, roughly sliced

3 cinnamon quills

6 green cardamom pods

7 cloves

2 tbsp ginger paste (see page 93)

2 tbsp garlic paste (see page 93)

6 green chillies, finely sliced

½ tsp turmeric powder

2 tsp chilli powder

1 tbsp ground coriander

200ml water

2kg skinless chicken on the bone, ideally 2 chickens quartered

1kg natural yoghurt, fork whipped and at room temperature (I like to use one with 10% fat but use low-fat yoghurt if you like)

3 large tomatoes, chopped

1 tbsp salt flakes

Big bunch of coriander and mint leaves, chopped

1kg basmati rice, rinsed, plus 4 litres water and a pinch of salt for cooking

Yellow food colouring

In a large pot, heat the oil to a medium temperature and fry the onions until see-through and blonde. Now drop in 2 cinnamon quills, 4 cardamom pods and 4 cloves and fry for 1–2 minutes until the spices darken and release their aroma. Spoon in the ginger and garlic pastes, plus the green chillies, turmeric, chilli powder and ground coriander along with the water, then stir well, mix everything and simmer for 4–5 minutes. Turn down the heat and add the chicken, browning on all sides for about 8–10 minutes until the meat starts to release its juices. Tip in the yoghurt and tomatoes, stirring constantly, and cook for about 4–6 minutes until the tomatoes become a bit pulpy and puréed and the yoghurt has become silky. Add the salt and coriander and mint leaves. Turn up the heat and cook for another 5 minutes, allowing all the ingredients to simmer and acquaint themselves with each other. Remove from the heat.

Using a separate stockpot filled with 4 litres of water, add a pinch of salt, 1 cinnamon quill, 2 green cardamom pods and 3 cloves and bring to a rolling simmer. Pour in the rice and boil until three-quarters cooked. Drain the rice.

Now to assemble the biryani. Remove the chicken pieces from the gravy with a slotted spoon. Using the same large pot, spread some of the chicken gravy at the bottom, cover with a layer of rice and sprinkle with few drops of yellow food colour-ing, take a few pieces of chicken and place on top of the rice. Spoon over some more gravy, then repeat these steps until you end up with a final coating of rice with some more gravy and food colouring over the top. Place a damp tea towel over the top of the pan and place the lid back on. Place the pot over a griddle pan or large frying pan on a low heat and steam the biryani for about 12–15 minutes until the rice is fluffy.

Tip out the contents on to a platter and jumble everything. The result should be a mix of yellow ochre rice, juicy chicken ready to fall off the bone and whole spices peering out of the rice mountain.

Serve with Mixed Sabzi (page 163) and Raitha (page 224).

METHI CHICKEN

Serves 4

7.5cm fresh root ginger, peeled and chopped
4 garlic cloves, chopped
Salt
2 tbsp lemon juice
3 tbsp water
4 skinless, boneless chicken breasts
4 tbsp olive oil
250ml natural yoghurt, fork whipped and at room temperature
    (I like to use one with 10% fat)
⅓ tsp garam masala (see page 46)

For the paste

2 medium tomatoes, chopped
150g fresh methi/fenugreek leaves (100g dried leaves –
    kasoori methi – if you can't get fresh)
3 green chillies, chopped
2 tsp tomato purée
50ml water

Blend the ginger, garlic and a generous pinch of salt with the lemon juice and water until smooth. Chop the chicken into cubes, cover with the lemon ginger marinade and refrigerate for an hour or more. Combine the paste ingredients and blitz.

Heat the oil in a pan over a high heat and fry the chicken, still covered in the marinade, browning on all sides for 10 minutes. Add in the fenugreek paste and cook for another 10 minutes, or until the oil starts to separate around the edge of the pan. Gently pour in the yoghurt, stirring to make sure it's assimilated. Sprinkle in the garam masala, cover and reduce the heat to low, cooking for a further 15 minutes, or until the chicken is springy and tender. Add water if it starts sticking.

Now tuck in and gobble down with soft hot Chapattis (page 172). It's also thoroughly mouth-watering served with Bayside Baingan (page 56).

'IT'S A WRAP'

The clapperboard snapped and the director called the words the crew had been waiting to hear for hours: 'It's a wrap.' A fourteen-hour day at Eastern Studios was filled with meticulous detail. The director clearly had an undiagnosed case of obsessive compulsive disorder and had been tediously commanding take after take, leaving the crew's resources depleted and desperate for an energy hit. The remedy was found in the city's street canteens where bowls of rice coupled with fresh curry would return vigour, good humour and camaraderie to the crew. Lawrie, a young man in his early twenties, had earned his stripes in the studios as a runner and learnt to choose the right moments to feed his colleagues with jokes and, in this case, when to dip into his dessert of choice – a shiny steel bowl of gajar ka halwa, a carrot reduction concentrated in whole milk, tenderly courted by pistachios and raisins. The vibrant orange texture, a fibrous semolina-like dessert, is a well-deserved treat – deliciously indulgent and perfect in the presence of friends. Like Lawrie Uncle, I find one bowl is never enough, two is about right and three is the definition of gluttony. I'm on the wrong side of two and I'm pretty sure you'll be joining me soon.

GAJAR KA HALWA

Serves up to 10

1 litre whole milk
1.5kg carrots, finely grated
200g sugar
100g butter

20 pistachio nuts,
   roughly crushed
3 tbsp raisins
2 tsp ground cardamom
   powder

In a large pan bring the milk to the boil, then turn down to simmer gently. Add the carrots (for speed, grate in a blender), stirring regularly until the carrots have become tender, the milk has evaporated and the mix is spongy. It will take around 30 minutes. Drop in the sugar and cook for at least 30 minutes until the sugar has dissolved and the milk is completely absorbed. Slide in the butter, glazing the carrot halwa with a deep sheen, stirring for another 5 minutes. Add the nuts, raisins and cardamom powder, thoroughly mixing together. Serve warm.

Carrot halwa will keep in a fridge for about a week, or you can freeze it for a couple of months. When you fancy indulging, just warm it up.

UAE BLOCKBUSTERS

With a swagger, Lawrie arrived on his own in Abu Dhabi, UAE in the mid-1970s, keen to reinvent himself and confine the past to memory. Now was his opportunity to shine, to become something, someone else, away from the preconceptions of home. He spread smiles as liberally as butter on hot chapattis, softening the hearts of the chain-smoking production lackeys at the film studios. In a highly class-structured culture, his approach was one of generous inclusion. He didn't care for rank, status, family background, shades of colour or religious inclination. All were equal and all were welcome. Long days at the studios led to sociable evenings in the shared immigrant film crew house and the smells from the kitchen had a language of their own. They would talk to him in dialects his ears were getting more and more acquainted with. There were the gentle tones of coconut and curry leaves – ahh, must be a Keralan fish stew – or the chitter-chatter of popping spices in hot skillets combined with vegetables, which indicated the dialogue of Tollas at work, or thoughtful and considered cardamom and coffee as the Parsis had their caffeine fix, or the rich scent of Punjabis working their magic with yoghurt and lamb.

Now it was Lawrie's turn to contribute to the conversation. It would be poetic, encouraging and down-to-earth. Accessing a family favourite, he'd cook shaljam ghosht, a marriage of earthy turnips and comforting lamb stew with the sonorous tones of juicy tomatoes.

This dish has a language of its own, both visual and verbal. If you are left with a craving for more and find yourself murmuring 'mmm', then Lawrie would be delighted that you'd understood and learnt the language of shaljam ghosht. All that's left to do is study some more and create it again.

SHALJAM GHOSHT

Serves 4–6

5 tbsp vegetable oil
2 large onions, sliced
5cm fresh root ginger, peeled and chopped
4 garlic cloves, smashed and chopped
4–6 green chillies, chopped and seeds retained
1 tsp paprika
1 tsp turmeric powder
2 tsp fennel seeds, pummelled and powdered
1 tbsp ground coriander
4 black cardamom pods
1 cinnamon quill
3 large tomatoes, roughly chopped
500ml water
1kg boneless lamb, chopped into chunks
Salt
500g turnips, chopped into chunks

Taking a large lidded pot or casserole dish, heat the oil over a low temperature and fry the onions until blonde for around 8–10 minutes. Add the ginger, garlic and chillies and stir fry for 3–4 minutes. Next, spoon in the paprika, turmeric, fennel and coriander, then drop in the cardamom pods, cinnamon quill, tomatoes and 50ml of the water. Mix everything thoroughly, cooking for 2 minutes until you have the base of a sauce. Tip in the lamb, turn up the heat to medium and jumble everything up, coating the meat with the spice base. Cover, turn the heat down and cook for about 15 minutes. The lamb will surrender its juices and the spices will bask.

Uncover and keep the pot cooking until the sauce has

dried a bit and is sticking to the lamb, then season with salt
and add the rest of the water. Cover and simmer for another
30 minutes, stirring regularly. Now tip in the turnips and
cook for another 20 minutes or until the turnips have become less identifiable and almost mushy – easy to crush with
the back of a spoon – and the meat is nice and tender.

The sweet earthiness of the turnips and lamb basted in
ingredients from the spice trail will leave an indelible mark
on your memory. Serve with rice and green peas, hot flatbread and a vegetable side.

PERSIAN BREW

The scent was an ancient one, striking elegant, nutty notes. Coffee beans were finely ground and mixed with crushed cardamom powder, sweetened by lumps of cane sugar and all vigorously stirred under the command of the Parsi lodgers. This brew is refined, elegant and speaks of a revered food culture.

COFFEE

Serves 2 mugs or 4 small cups

4 tbsp filter coffee (depending how strong you like it)
12 green cardamom pods, seeds removed and crushed
   into powder
Milk, to taste
Lumps of sugar to sweeten the ceremony

Scoop the coffee into a '6 cup' cafetière, adding boiling water according to the strength you prefer. Mix in the cardamom powder and leave to stand for a couple of minutes before plunging. Serve with milk and sugar to taste.

THE FOOD OF KERALA

The Keralans, from India's southern state, possess a different way with fish, a familiarity and respect which Lawrie hadn't experienced in his home ocean city of Karachi. They prepared snacks such as crunchy pakoras and delicious delicate stews partnered with rice, perfect for food on the hoof especially when served in tiffin boxes. These dishes have got me hook, line and sinker.

KERALAN FISH STEW

Serves 4

1kg haddock fillets
Juice of 2 fat limes
Salt flakes
3 tbsp vegetable oil
400ml can of coconut milk
6cm fresh root ginger, peeled and finely chopped
6 green chillies, deseeded and chopped
Handful of curry leaves

For the fish stew base
1 tsp fennel seeds
2 tsp coriander seeds
1 tsp cumin seeds
2 tbsp desiccated coconut
2 tbsp cashew nuts
1 large onion, chopped roughly
4 green chillies, chopped, seeds retained
4 garlic cloves, smashed
2 tbsp coriander leaves

Slice the fish into bite-size chunks and place in a dish, then dab with some of the lime juice and sprinkle with salt flakes. Cover and cool in the fridge for an hour.

Don't spend your time smashing and pounding the ingredients for the base, just pop everything in a blender and pulse to make a paste.

In a large pan or wok, heat the oil over a lowish heat, scoop in the fish stew base and fry for 4–5 minutes until you see the oil splitting from the curry. Take off the heat and stir in the coconut milk, then introduce ginger, green chillies, the rest of the lime juice, curry leaves and a touch more salt. Return to the heat and simmer for 5 minutes, allowing the fish stew base to coalesce. Add the fish and cook for 6–8 minutes until it's firm but not flaky.

Serve with a helping of rice.

TOLLYWOOD

A long way from their native Tolla dialect in Tamil Nadu, with their now-famous film industry rivalling the Bollywood behemoth, these east-coast travellers knocked together tangy vegetable dishes cut with plenty of heat and popping spices. They widened Lawrie's experience of subcontinent Indian food, allowing him to taste places he'd never had the pleasure of visiting.

TOLLYWOOD VEGETABLES

Serves 4

3 medium-sized sweet potatoes, peeled and diced
2 green chillies, finely sliced
⅓ tsp turmeric powder
Salt
150ml water

For the masala

1 tbsp coriander seeds
2 tsp cumin seeds
2 tbsp desiccated coconut
1 tsp fennel seeds

For the popping spices

3 tbsp vegetable oil
1 tsp mustard seeds
1 tsp cumin seeds
1 tsp sesame seeds

Over a medium temperature, heat the masala ingredients in a pan until the seeds turn a shade darker and they cede their scent. Remove from the heat and leave to cool. You have two options here – either blend in a spice grinder or pound in a pestle and mortar until powder.

In a large pan over a medium heat, warm the oil for the popping spices, then drop in the seeds. As soon as they start to burst, add the main recipe ingredients: the potatoes, chillies and turmeric. Stir to coat everything, and add a touch of salt. Decant the water into the pan, bring to the boil, then reduce the heat, and cover and simmer for around 15 minutes until the potatoes are cooked (stab with a fork and it should easily slide through). The dish should be on the dry side. Sprinkle in the masala powder, stir, cover and remove from the heat, leaving it to rest for 2 minutes.

Serve with Sweet and Sour Tomato Chutney (page 87).

Welcome to Southall

ਜੀ ਆਇਆਂ ਨੂੰ, ਸਾਉਥਾਲ

GUPSHUP PLATES

Like the rest of his brothers, Lawrie had wanderlust. An eastern wind blew him across Europe and he breezed into Britain and set up camp in Southall, West London, or Little India as it's affectionately known. In some ways the apple hasn't fallen too far from the tree. He left the film industry with bitter-sweet emotions to be closer to his family, excited to be reunited with his brothers, yet melancholic about his departure from the studios. His is a poetic, sometimes mournful life, yet his chipper disposition navigates him through troubled waters. He's a devotee of his homeland, which is perhaps why Southall, with its familiar smells of kebabs, pakoras and samosas and sights of turbans, saris, prayer caps and brown skin, sets him at ease. Little India is packed with places to eat – chaat houses, cafés, restaurants, stalls – and, if that's not enough, simply make some friends and you'll be invited in for supper quicker than you can accept. The chaat house was the place to trade *gupshup* (chit-chat) and while away time over easy food, starting with spiced snacks such as Channa Chaat (page 216) and Onion Bhajiya (page 215). Then, depending on whether one had a place to be, snacks would morph into light meals and possibly a visit to Glassy Junction, the only pub in the UK to accept Indian rupees. Gupshup dishes are reflective of a state of mind. They are plates of food to ponder over while banishing the speed of modern life. It's food for friends.

Pooris (see page 28) are a staple in chaat houses, and make for tasty gupshup sessions. They are delicious eaten with snacks and vegetable dishes, such as chickpeas, daals, dry potato curries or feisty pickles.

ONION BHAJIYA

Serves 6 or more as a snack

150g gram (chickpea) flour
Water
½ tsp bicarbonate of soda
2 tsp cumin seeds
2 tsp nigella seeds
Salt
5–6 large onions, finely sliced
Vegetable oil for frying

In a big bowl, tip in the flour and add enough water to create a thick batter. Sprinkle in the bicarbonate of soda and both types of seeds plus some salt seasoning. Put in the onions and mix well.

Using a large wok or deep frying pan, pour in the oil to a depth of 2–3cm and heat to a medium-high temperature. Drop in a cumin seed and if it sizzles like a maniac the oil's ready. Use a ladle and gently lower in spoonfuls of the mix. Fry for around 4 minutes until golden brown. Use a slotted spoon and remove the bhajiya, then drain on kitchen paper.

Serve hot and with a dipping chutney of your choice

CHANNA CHAAT

Serves 2–4 as a snack

2 tbsp olive oil
1 large onion, sliced
5cm fresh root ginger, peeled and finely chopped
400g tin of pre-boiled chickpeas
2 medium tomatoes, diced
1 tsp sugar
1 tsp salt flakes (less if regular salt)
2 tsp chaat masala (see page 219)
50ml lemon juice
A palmful of coriander leaves, roughly chopped
2 green chillies, finely chopped

You can eat this cold or hot. The cool, salad version simply requires that you mix everything in a large bowl, cover, refrigerate and eat 3–4 hours later.

The hot version is pretty quick too. Using a large frying pan, heat the oil over a medium temperature and fry the onion until passive, quickly followed by the ginger and chillies cooking for 2–3 minutes before adding the chickpeas. Sauté everything for another 3 minutes, sneak in the tomatoes and turn up the heat. Sprinkle in the sugar and salt and cook for another 3 minutes. Take off the heat, dust with chaat masala, douse in lemon, mix well and scatter with coriander leaves. Done.

Serve with soft Pooris (page 28).

ACCESSORIES

Think of chaat masala as the spice sprinkle that has the power to give most dishes a makeover. The merest dash dusted over salads and relishes completely enriches them, bringing notes of sour warmth and a gentle intensity. Once blended it can keep for weeks to months in an airtight jar, but as with all spices it loses its vibrancy if retained for too long. It's better to create smaller quantities, and often. Chaat masala's cornucopia of whole spices may look daunting but the result is transformational and quicker than you think.

Sabzi pickle is a mixed vegetable pickle and another key accessory. It is sharp, tasty and heavily textured, and goes well with pooris, other flatbreads and with dry curries such as Lamb Bhuna (page 222) or Guddu Chicken (page 92).

CHAAT MASALA

Makes enough to dress more than 12 dishes

Ingredients to toast
1 tbsp cumin seeds
2 tsp fennel seeds
1 tsp ajwain seeds (carom seeds)
2 dried red chillies, partially slit to stop from exploding
1 tbsp coriander seeds
½ tbsp black peppercorns
1 tsp cardamom powder
Pinch asafoetida powder

Ingredients to tip into the blender
1 tbsp garam masala (see page 46)
1 tbsp mango powder (amchur)
½ tbsp black salt (it's a bit sulphurous so easy does it)
1 tsp chilli powder
½ tbsp sea salt flakes
1 tsp cloves
1 tsp ground cinnamon

In a large pan over a moderate heat, tip in the ingredients to toast (apart from the asafoetida) and dry-roast for 2 minutes or until the ingredients turn a darker shade and they cede their scent. Now add the asafoetida to the pan and heat through for 40 seconds. Turn out the ingredients into a bowl and leave to cool.

Using a blender, spice grinder, or pestle and mortar if you're up for the muscle power, combine all the toasted spices and the remaining ingredients and pound into a fine powder. The result will be a reddish-brown crush ready to scatter on any dish that needs a little pep talk.

SABZI PICKLE

Makes at least 8 servings

2 medium carrots, peeled and diced
180g cauliflower, cut into bite-size florets
1 onion, cut into chunks
Salt
2 tbsp olive oil
2 garlic cloves, sliced into flakes
3cm fresh root ginger, peeled and sliced wafer-thin
4 green chillies, finely sliced
1 tsp dark mustard seeds
¼ tsp turmeric powder
½ tsp paprika
1 tsp crushed coriander seeds
Quarter of a cucumber, diced into small chunks
½ tsp sugar
200ml cider vinegar

Pop the carrots, cauliflower and onion into a bowl, sprinkle with salt, then cover and set aside in a cool place. Leave overnight if possible.

Using a large pan, heat the oil to a medium temperature and slide in the garlic, ginger, chillies, coriander and mustard seeds. When the seeds start to crack and burst, add the turmeric and paprika, stir all the ingredients and fry for 1 minute. Add all the vegetables (minus the cucumber) to the pan, stir to coat everything thoroughly and fry for 4 minutes. Remove from the heat and leave to cool. Mix in the cucumber and sprinkle in the sugar. Using an airtight glass jar, ideally one with a rubber seal, decant all the ingredients and pour in the vinegar. Seal and leave to stand for a couple of hours before eating. Alternatively, refrigerate and use within 4 weeks.

LAWRIE UNCLE'S BHUNA

'I'm gay. Thought you should know.'

It was an unusual time for my cousin to come out, given it was the wake of his mother, my auntie Doreen, whose Cockney charm was robbed by cancer. The house was bursting with Asian mourners who, as tradition dictated, were wailing upon arrival and then tucking into the food, which was feisty and irresistible. With his brilliant eyes and soft nature, my cousin, accompanied by his partner, spoke of his mother in a gentle and touching tone.

Uncle Lawrie's eyebrows arched into an exaggerated expression at his nephew's news. He was oblivious to the hands patting his back in gratitude at the lamb bhuna he'd prepared for this occasion as he tried to process the announcement.

'Brother, *bawth achar hé* [Brother, it's very good],' someone congratulated Lawrie on his bhuna offering. Recognising that now wasn't the time to discuss sexual orientation, I seized the opportunity, employing distraction. I diverted Lawrie Uncle just as he attempted to begin the discussion and asked him how he made the mutton bhuna so incredibly tender. It was packed with peppery spices yet, unlike the gravy-based masala dishes, it was dry, with the masala clinging to the meat like newly acquainted lovers. The story behind Lawrie's bhuna began some fifty years earlier, and he took me back to the streets of Karachi as he described chunks of lamb and whole spices being browned (bhuna'd) in large frying pans, then flooded with spice reduced to a fierce concentration of onion, garlic, ginger, and a wardrobe of cumin and fennel seeds that stuck to the mutton tighter than Tom Jones's trousers. This dry dish would be eaten with steaming hot chapattis or used as a filling in tender, thin flatbread and consumed as a wrap on the go. Lawrie's eyes darted across to my cousin, who was just about to dive into a plate of bhuna, and with the dexterity of a Punjabi goat he leapt from his seat.

'No! *Puther* [son/nephew], you want to eat that with some *dhey* [yoghurt]. It tastes better.'

Generations apart yet united by food, the bhuna negotiated the distance between them. Acceptance, understanding and hunger brokered a joint mission: devour the lamb before it disappeared.

Try this with Aloo and Moti Mirch (page 59) or a side of Sabzi Pickle (page 220).

LAMB MUTTON BHUNA

Serves 6

1 tbsp ground coriander
½ tsp clove powder
¼ tsp chilli powder
20ml water
100ml vegetable oil
3 black cardamom pods
1 cinnamon quill
1 tsp black peppercorns
1 tsp coriander seeds
1 tsp cumin seeds
1 tsp fennel seeds
3 small onions, sliced

1 tbsp ginger paste (see page 93)
1 tbsp garlic paste (see page 93)
4 green chillies, finely chopped
Salt
1kg mutton on the bone, cut into pieces (it's tastier on the bone, but you can substitute boneless pieces if preferred)
300ml hot water

In a bowl, combine the coriander, clove, chilli and water.

Like a wilful child, bhuna needs a lot of attention, but it's a spirited dish. In a large stewing pot, heat the oil over a medium temperature and fry the cardamom pods, cinnamon quill, peppercorns, and coriander, cumin and fennel seeds until they tap-dance and darken. Drop in the onions and cook until they gain a buttery appearance. Add the ginger and garlic pastes and chillies, and muddle in the spice powder mixture you made earlier. Cook with salt for a couple of minutes until the musk rises and traces your nostrils. Turn the heat down and introduce the mutton, browning for 30 minutes, adding a little of the water to stop it sticking if necessary. Flood the pot with the hot water and whack up the heat to bubbling, then turn down the temperature and simmer for 30 minutes, allowing the gravy to thicken. Now increase the heat, turn over the meat regularly for another 20–30 minutes, so that it browns or 'bhunas' and the oil separates out.

This dish is feisty, memorable and bold. Serve with Chapattis (page 172) and Raitha (page 224).

CUCUMBER AND TOMATO RAITHA

Makes enough for 10–12 servings

300ml natural yoghurt, at room temperature (I like to use one
 with 10% fat)
Half a cucumber, diced
3 plump tomatoes, roughly chopped
Pinch of salt
1 tsp cumin seeds
Paprika, for dusting

Fork-whip the yoghurt, then add the cucumber, tomatoes
and salt. Just before serving, toast the cumin seeds in a pan
until just brown, not smoking, and sprinkle on top. Dust
with a little paprika for flourish.

SECRETS

All families possess secrets. Some are kept for ever, some are stumbled upon, others simply remain a conundrum. With seven children, there were simply more secrets for my father's family to harbour, and Lawrie had his fair share – although one could argue that his weren't so much secrets as mysteries, knowledge unshared. For some this can arouse mild feelings of jealousy, for others it provokes respect and admiration for something beyond their ability. I detected the latter when chatting to Lawrie's other partner in crime, Guddu Chachu. When quizzed about his brother's prowess in the kitchen, he instantly recalled Lawrie's fish biryani. 'I don't know how he does it, but his fish biryani is stunning. I don't know how he keeps the fish from breaking up, but it's pukka.' He's not alone in his proclamation. Other family testimonials point to his biryani as a dish of expertise. To date the recipe has remained a secret, but, like a set of ancient hieroglyphics, here the mystery has been decoded for your delectation.

FISH BIRYANI

Serves 4 healthy portions and a bit more

For the rice
500g white rice, rinsed
   (optional soak for 30
   minutes, then drained)
1 litre water
6 cloves
1 tbsp crushed coriander
   seeds
2 tsp cumin seeds

For the fish
1kg boneless firm white fish,
   such as cod, king fish or
   coley
Juice of 3 limes
1 tbsp salt flakes
1 tsp turmeric
6 tbsp vegetable oil

For the curry base
6 tbsp vegetable oil
2 onions, sliced
5 tomatoes, chopped
4 green chillies, sliced
2 tbsp ginger paste (see page
   93)
2 tbsp garlic paste (see page
   93)
½ tsp turmeric powder
1 tsp chilli powder
1 tbsp ground coriander
6 green cardamom pods
200ml water

To finish
Yellow food colouring
Bunch of mint leaves

The key with this recipe is to make sure the fish doesn't break up too much, and to gently layer the rice with the curried gravy and fish.

Step 1: Prepare the rice. In a large pot, bring the water to the boil and then add the rice and the other ingredients, apart from the yellow food colouring. Cook the rice until it's 75 per cent done and still a bit nutty. Different varieties of rice means cooking times vary. Drain the rice and transfer it to a platter.

Step 2: Cut the fish into largish pieces (about 8cm long).

In a large metallic bowl, mix the lime juice, salt and turmeric together, add the fish pieces, cover and refrigerate for at least an hour. Then warm the oil in a large frying pan and fry the fish until golden brown and firm, being careful not to overcook and let it become flaky. Using a slotted spoon, remove the fish and drain on kitchen paper.

Step 3: For the curry base, heat the oil in a large, deep frying pan over a medium setting. Add the onions and cook until soft and bronzed. Tip in the tomatoes and chillies, ginger and garlic pastes, and fry for 3–4 minutes until the ingredients are sizzling gently. Then, one at a time, stir in the turmeric, chilli and coriander. Drop in the cardamom pods and simmer for a couple of minutes before adding the water. Mix everything well, reduce the heat to low and cook for 10 minutes or until the tomatoes have turned into a rough purée and the oil has risen to the surface. Cover and remove from the heat.

Step 4: Assemble the biryani. Using the same pot you cooked the rice in, spread some of the curry base (the gravy) at the bottom, cover with a layer of rice, add a few drops of yellow food colouring, then put some fish pieces on top. Cover with some more gravy, then repeat the process until you have a final layer of rice with gravy, adding some food colouring drops. Sprinkle the mint leaves on top.

Place a damp tea towel over the top of the pan and place the lid back on. Place the pot over a griddle pan or large frying pan on a low heat and steam the fish biryani for about 10 minutes until the rice is fluffy.

Gently spoon out the ingredients on to a large platter, taking care not to break the fish. The heap of rice, curry gravy and fish should be a riotous mix of white, yellow and deep sienna.

Serve with Mixed Sabzi (page 163) and Raitha (page 224).

ALWAYS BETTER TOGETHER

Rarity is often celebrated, feted and prized. In our family's case it's a rare occasion when all the brothers are gathered together, and it's cherished as a special time for the family. Fat smiles are spread easily, young and old interact and the brothers exchange banter and recall their life in Pakistan, mim-icking friends and family members for laughs. As the evening progresses, the screwcap to a single malt is released and the storytelling continues, with Lawrie leading the way, creating a dramatic hush leading to a punchline crescendo. Equally rare to the brothers' gathering is the dish created to celebrate their union. It's unique in its individuality and is highly regarded as a delicacy. The intense saffron-looking gravy is rumoured to be so packed with nutrients that it's nature's way to ward off maladies such as the common cold. It's a recipe that releases their inner child, and for a moment we glimpse four boys eating a dish reserved for special times. The wobbly flesh of paya (lamb's feet) is bathed in a rich curried base and peeled apart with fresh, hot chapattis. The reminiscing continues, but this time no words are exchanged, just the sound of memories being exhumed and shared over food reflective of their lives. A shared childhood, adult lives sometimes apart, but always better when together.

Paya is an adventure in food. It's not a well-trodden path, but it's invigorating to try something unfamiliar.

PAYA

Serves 4

4 sheep or goat trotters (you'll find these in Asian butchers)
1 tbsp rice flour
Salt
250ml water
150ml olive oil
1 tsp cumin seeds
2 onions, finely chopped
5cm fresh root ginger, peeled and grated
3 garlic cloves, crushed
2 tbsp lemon juice
400g tin of chopped tomatoes
2 green chillies, finely chopped
1 tsp turmeric powder
1 tsp garam masala (see page 46)
½ tsp cayenne pepper

Rinse the trotters (paya) thoroughly and chop each one into 2 pieces. Using a bowl, rub the trotters in rice flour and salt, then rinse once again. Bring the water to the boil in a large pot and place the trotters in the water with a sprinkling of salt. Lower the heat and simmer for 90 minutes, adding water where necessary to stop the pan from drying out.

Using a separate frying pan or wok, pour in the oil and heat over a medium temperature. Add the cumin seeds and, when they start to sizzle, introduce the onions, ginger and garlic, frying for 3–4 minutes. Lower the heat and add the tomatoes, chillies, turmeric, garam masala and cayenne pepper, plus a dash of salt, and cook until the oil rises to the surface. It'll take around 10–15 minutes.

Now add the trotters and the stock they've been simmering in and cook for another 4–5 minutes. Tip in the lemon juice.

The result should be a bright orangey dish which can served with plain white rice and hot flatbread. Unlike any recipe you'll encounter in an Indian restaurant, it's a voyage into a part of Indian subcontinent food that's rarely explored.

RUBBER-BANDING
OVER RICE DESSERT

Professional psychologists call it 'rubber-banding', a moment, a feeling, an action which, when experienced, pings us back to a previous time in life when we experienced the same emotion, as if it's happening all over again. For Lawrie and his now silver thatch of hair, badaam phirni is the dessert that follows his childhood, adolescent, adult and senior years. It's a relationship that has stood the test of time and it still tastes as beguiling and comforting as the first day he tried it. Maybe it's the soft milky texture combined with the nutritious depth of ground almonds and ground rice flour, crowned with the regal scent of cardamom powder, which has kept his taste buds so loyal for all these years. Badaam phirni captured Lawrie a long time ago. I've since become a disciple and I think it's time you joined the movement.

BADAAM PHIRNI

Serves 4–6

20 almonds or 4 tbsp flaked almonds
600ml whole milk
4 tbsp rice flour
4 tbsp unrefined sugar
10 saffron strands
1 tsp cardamom powder
12 crushed pistachios

In a pan of hot water, blanch the almonds and remove the skin. Alternatively, use flaked almonds. Use a hand blender to grind the almonds in 120ml of the milk to produce a paste. Transfer to a bowl and mix in the rice flour.

In a saucepan, bring the rest of the milk to the boil and tip in the sugar, stirring until it dissolves. Spoon out 1 tbsp hot milk into a small bowl and lace the saffron through it until the milk has taken on the colour of the strands. Strain the saffron milk back into the saucepan and add the almond paste. Gently stir until the mix thickens and becomes creamy, then shake in the cardamom powder. Remove from the heat and leave to cool, then sprinkle the crushed pistachios over the dessert and refrigerate for an hour or so before serving.

This delicious, light dessert is best presented in cute bowls and served with little spoons – you will want every mouthful to last!

A JOURNEY OFF THE EATEN TRACK

These curry memoirs have been quite a journey. Cast across seven decades, they are stories that have illuminated the past, and uncovered joy, tragedy, dreams, struggle, adventure, love and the ever-present role of simple home-cooked food. For me, writing this book has been a personal discovery of my family history and the uniting role of food.

These recipes have fused family gatherings, fuelled the immigrant work ethic and delighted the palates of our family's offspring. This book isn't just about nutrition, it's about nourishment at every level. It's about food to fill your senses and bellies and spark a lust for adventure. It's a selfless act to cook for others, entirely to please and satiate their epicurean desires, and that's the spirit of curry: like these stories it's a cuisine that is meant to be shared, generous in taste and plentiful in measure. This is an inheritance I've wanted to share for a while and, as they say, history is simply a prologue for the future, so curry is here to stay … anyone hungry?

URBAN RAJAH'S CURRY MEMOIRS
SOCIAL ENTERPRISE COMMENTARY

The Urban Rajah is committed to helping charities working in India to liberate people caught in the human trafficking chain or forced into bonded labour as well as supporting grass roots charities who feed, educate and care for children who are born into India's slums. As a result, a percentage of author royalties from this book will be donated by the Urban Rajah to support these organisations. His pop-up restaurant Cash n Curry also operates as a social enterprise, guests are treated to an Indian feast and pay what they think its worth. All profits go towards helping transform the lives of those trapped in poverty in India. The Urban Rajah's philosophy is simple: entertain, feed and transform.

THANKS

Wow … what a ride it's been, like a Karachi bus, packed with adventure, sometimes a bit shaky but eventually you arrive. The trip, however, wouldn't have been possible or the least bit enjoyable without the support, encouragement and belief of some of my nearest and dearest.

To my exquisite wife Jeanne (aka the Maharani), thanks for all your patience, food tasting, love and dedication, I couldn't have made it without you gorgeous. Sorry for all tardy time-keeping but in Guddu Chachu's words you can *never hurry a curry*.

Mum, you're a true beauty and in my eyes one of the original *Spice Girls*. Thanks for your steadfastness, confidence and hope, I am, however, still scarred from the checked flares you clad me in as a kid. My big brother, Ian, thank you for taking it easy on me as a kid and being there through thick and thin, hopefully you'll discover a few more recipes to try your hand at beyond Keema Aloo.

To Dad (The VP), the original Karachi kid who's taken curry to California. Thanks for your belief in me and all your culinary inspiration and gastronomic advice as well as the family stories … you started this whole thing off and look where it's got us! To the Silver Foxes, my uncles, Albert, Lawrence and Stanley, thanks for keeping the curry faith all these years and indulging me in sublime food ever since I was in short trousers. I owe my spice horizons to you and your signature dishes, but don't think the voyage ends here – I'll be over soon enough for another helping. To those who were a special part of the journey and will be with me for ever, Dhadha-Ji, Dhadhi-Ji (Mama), Nana, Nani, Uncle John, Auntie Doreen, Sharron and Uncle Ikram. Big up to the rest of the Peters clan, you know who you are!

A special thank you to my brilliant agent, Amanda Preston, and the team at LBA for backing me and helping me to live the dream, you're awesome. Let's do more good stuff. (Credit is due to Jen and Justin Hammond at My Life In Art for the intro.) Thank you, thank you, thank you to the talented Headline Publishing All Stars: Sarah Emsley for your insight, encouragement and making it happen, Richard Roper, Patrick Insole (creative champion), Veronique Norton, Lynsey Sutherland and Kim Hardie for all your hard work and patience.

A bear hug and a mwah mwah to my friends: Alex Gough for her brilliant scamps and illustrations, and Philipp 'The Fig' Figueroa for his film-making prowess, and to my creative superheroes: Tappers (Kevin Taplin at TenSevenNine) and Jimbo Williams for always inspiring me.

Finally thank you for buying my book.

INDEX

243

PICTURE CREDITS